IN THE SPIRIT OF

ASPEN

This book is dedicated to the people I loved who loved to ski and opened up the thrilling beauty of the Rocky Mountain West for me.

And to Mary and Bill Martin, without whose support and insiders' view this book could not exist.

© 2002 Assouline Publishing
601 West 26th Street, 18th floor
New York, NY 10001
USA
Tel.: 212 989-6810   Fax: 212 647-0005
www.assouline.com

Copyedited by Caitlin Leffel

ISBN: 2 84323 399 2

Color separation: Gravor (Switzerland)
Printed by Grafiche Milani (Italy)

KATHRYN LIVINGSTON

IN THE SPIRIT OF

ASPEN

ASSOULINE

"Everything I have given to skiing has been returned tenfold . . ."
—*Friedl Pfeifer*, Nice Goin'

Contents

PAGES 6-7: *At America's premier winter playground, Aspen's gridlike streets intersect with Aspen Mountain's fabulous downhill runs. Beyond these lie the Buttermilk, Aspen Highlands, and Snowmass Village ski complexes.*

Introduction

Many describe their first visit to Aspen, Colorado, as simply "a case of chemistry." They experience an intense physical attraction and emotional pull. The combination of the startling, jagged mountain horizon, the magnetic mix of Victorian and contemporary architecture, the alluring danger of exciting ski runs and whitewater streams, the tempo of youth and vigor in the streets, the scent of money in the air combined with a sprinkling of sex and play, all add up to an appeal that is both heart-tugging and visceral. Coming to Aspen for the first time is like a first encounter with a potential lover: It appears so thoroughly original, so distractingly complex—part international sophisticate, part solidly rooted American rustic—that the passion inspired in a single moment will either quickly fizzle out or become a lifetime love affair.

It has been said that Aspen is more a fantasy, a happening, an attitude, than an actual geographic location. But tucked into an inaccessible corner of a Rocky Mountain valley, some 222 miles southwest of Denver and almost 8,000 feet above Wall Street, Aspen does exist as a unique, natural paradise, filled with all the luscious, modern luxuries one could possibly desire. The town of Aspen is laid out in a neat, orderly grid of streets, not unlike that of Manhattan. Yet very few of the diverse elements that make Aspen so special fit together as squarely and easily. An idyllic meeting of classic Victorian and Wild West, this storybook village of around 7,000 year-round residents swells to about 130,000 in high season. Between Christmas and New Year's and again in February and March, Aspen becomes America's biggest and most glamorous winter playground as jet setters and ski bums alike descend in droves to take advantage of the sensational skiing on four separate mountain complexes. With plenty of fresh powder blanketing the downhill trails by November, the winter season kicks off at Thanksgiving when the World Cup races bring skiing's most famous international champions to town. By mid-December, private jets start to pour in from around the world as affluent celebrities and scene-seekers make their annual pilgrimage to Aspen from the urban jungles of New York, Los Angeles, Europe, South America, and the Middle East. It is a running joke in Aspen that the Gulfstreams and Learjets lined up on the runway of tiny Sardy Field sometimes outnumber the cars in the parking lot of Aspen airport as the private plane increasingly becomes the vehicle of choice for Aspen's annual visitors. Long known as a getaway for the rich and famous, over the years the Aspen area has been the stomping ground of such international titans as Lester Crown, Rupert Murdoch, and Gerald Hines, real-estate tycoons Donald Trump and Steve Tisch, Hollywood producers Merv Adelson and Peter Guber, Broadway producer Marty Richards, talk-show mogul Oprah Winfrey, oilmen Robert Mosbacher and David Koch, financiers George Soros and Ted Forstmann, and high-profile corporate chiefs Leonard Lauder and Michael Eisner. It is also the former home of late pop singer John Denver and current home of outlaw author Hunter S. Thompson. And, of course, Aspen today brims seasonally with Hollywood's leading men and women, including Jack Nicholson, Kevin Costner, Will Smith, Melanie Griffith and Antonio

Banderas, Goldie Hawn and Kurt Russell, and Michael Douglas and Catherine Zeta-Jones. During the holiday season, Aspen lights up even more when high-wattage stars such as Milla Jovovich, Ben Affleck, and Val Kilmer snowboard during the day and dance the night away at the Caribou Club, reveling in the anonymity of the secluded location and the sublime postcard beauty of the snow-heaped gingerbread houses. Yet while Aspen visually, geographically, and climactically offers a respite from Hollywood's sun-scorched landscape, it still wields such amenities as beautiful hotels, gourmet food, luxury spas, and a collection of boutiques that rival those of Madison Avenue, Rodeo Drive, or Via Montenapoleone. Like the best films, Aspen offers visitors an escape from the frenzied grind of daily life without straying too far from the reality they know.

Aspen has been an elite winter hideaway since the 1940s, when the likes of Gary Cooper, Lana Turner, and Ray Milland came to gambol in the snow and seek fashionable fun in the fresh mountain air. In addition to its reputation as a winter wonderland, however, Aspen has recently gained tremendous stature as an important year-round cultural mecca. The Aspen Institute, the Aspen Design Conference, the Anderson Ranch Art Program, the Aspen Music Festival, the Food and Wine Festival, Jazz Aspen, the Film Fest and the Aspen–Santa Fe Ballet all draw top international musicians, artists, and luminaries of architectural design as well as leaders of society, fashion, science, and politics. These factors make Aspen a must-hit destination for the contemporary jet set.

Aspen itself, however, has long been ambivalent about its cosmopolitan side. Measures such as its controversial "no growth" policy desperately aim to preserve its tranquility and natural qualities but are under constant attack from the increasing number of paved roads, condominium developments, and eclectic, eccentric expressions of modern architecture.

Though this eternal bickering over real-estate laws causes some to prophesy that soon Aspen will be inhabited only by aging billionaires, today that is clearly not the case. Energetic, ambitious young people are everywhere, tearing down Spar Gulch at 70 mph in sub-zero

PAGE 9: *Before political correctness swept Aspen, furs and cigarettes were sported with aplomb. Here, two spectators bundle up in fox and mink to watch the international racers compete in the January Wintersköl festivities, circa 1982.*

PAGE 10: *On a perfect spring morning in 1965, a first-time skier snowplows down the Buttermilk ski area.*

ABOVE: *Arriving via their private Gulfstream at Aspen's Sardy Field, a group of Chicagoans anticipate their sociable and sportive annual pilgrimage, circa 1980.*

PAGE 14: *Pyrotechnic displays and torchlight parades are part of Aspen's many exuberant celebrations. This fireworks display celebrates the World Cup races around Thanksgiving.*

PAGE 15: *The world's top skiers take part in three days of grueling competition at speeds in excess of 70mph for America's Downhill on Aspen Mountain, one of many international races televised from Aspen.*

weather during the "24 Hours of Aspen Marathon," defying gravity on snowshoes and skis for "America's Uphill," and engaging in extreme skiing feats of all kinds during the strenuous "X-Games." Sporting bloods from all over the world flock to Aspen for the wealth of physical challenges it offers. Two things are common to every visitor: Each would like to make Aspen's awesome natural environment his home someday and each has a story. The young man from Chile who drives the hotel's airport shuttle has a Ph.D. The quiet local rancher who takes Prince Bandar of Saudi Arabia on packhorse adventures and snowmobile rides is a descendant of the first judge in Western Colorado. A former fashion model from Mexico City who runs a tiny a residential hotel once found Princess Diana with Princes William and Harry standing in the doorway looking for a room.

What is it about Aspen that makes it so compelling to so many different types of people? How does this town continue to thrive year after snow-capped year with new, pulsating energy, without falling victim to the plagues of kitsch, passé or—worst of all—fake? Of all the rarefied international resorts, Aspen is the most invested with expectations of pleasure and peacefulness, cerebral stimulus and corporeal challenge, sociability and solitude. There may never be agreement in Aspen on land use, design, or development rules, but there is consensus on the fact that something special thrives in this place.

That something is Aspen's particular Western heritage and the earthy diligence of the diverse people who always have worked hard to make a living here. Before the area found fame in the ephemeral commodities of snow and culture, silver culled from the mountains by the ancestors of these Aspen natives first put this area on the map. To this day, the last rollicking decibels of Aspen at play fade away as the first clanging, scraping sounds of working Aspen begin at dawn. These are the grounded natives who wait for the yearly return of the bluebird, people whose identity comes from always having worked hard to keep their Rocky Mountain roots. And despite the constant influx of fresh people with fresh ideas from the East Coast, West Coast and continents beyond, the town still belongs to the locals. As part-time Aspen resident and longtime Aspen observer actor George Hamilton commented: "This is still a Stetson and blue-jeans town. It's not how rich and famous you are but how many locals you know that counts. It's an insiders' town and everybody wants to be on the inside. One of Aspen's most appealing aspects is that circles overlap, a great variety of people meet, get to talk. Whether it's a myth or not, Aspenites like to believe they have a classless society here."

Today, as always, Aspen is a mercurial, pioneering town, continuously evolving from one season to the next like the accumulation and melting of its legendary champagne powder. Embellished both by pastel Victorian facades and futuristic glass-and-stone mansions, Aspen is a confluence point of small-town values and big-city sensibilities. It's remote and individualistic. Though Aspen may seem caught in an interminable identity struggle, there is poignancy to its eternal growing pains. Ever a frontier town, Aspen exists always in a state of siege where settlers battle the invaders for control of the land. Yet what makes Aspen remarkable in today's commercially jaded social landscape is that it is a place where people from all walks of life still take time to contemplate and enjoy their zest for nature, art, and life itself.

Origins

Aspen began as a silver mining bonanza when, on Independence Day of 1879, two prospectors crossed over the treacherous high reaches of the Colorado Rockies near the Continental Divide. They struck gold at a distant alpine basin close to the headwaters of a pristine valley. Here, the river ran with such ferocity and noise, crashing rock against rock, that they called it Roaring Fork. In honor of the holiday, they named their mining claim "Independence."

At this time, Colorado was a brand new state, a member of the United States for only three years. The Civil War had ended only fifteen years earlier. Alexander Graham Bell and Thomas Edison had made discoveries that would soon revolutionize the way people lived. Thirty years had passed since the California Gold Rush, and miners had developed the technology and expertise essential to recognizing geological formations that could reveal hidden mineral deposits. Colorado was abuzz with rumors of mineral riches and the Rocky Mountains teemed with men from Philadelphia, Cincinnati, and New York who sought to invest in new wealth-producing pastures.

The two prospectors Charles E. Bennett and Philip W. Pratt were among the first white men ever to make the arduous

PAGE 18: *One of the most photographed unspoiled sites in North America—a favorite of trekkers and climbers—the Maroon Bell Wilderness Area south of Aspen is a source of spiritual renewal for all.*

PAGE 19: *The Round-Up Riders of the Rockies on their annual round-up: Two weeks of backpacking in the mountain wilderness of western Colorado "without women and with all the booze you can drink."*

ABOVE: *A relic from Aspen's silver mining days—the weathered old ore bin at the Durant Mine, photographed in 1952.*

OPPOSITE: *Heaped with snow, one of the typical Victorian cottages belonging to a worker in the mines.*

72-mile journey from the mining camp of Leadville to what is now the Aspen area. Arriving on horseback with packhorses in tow, they climbed the chilly 12,095-foot summit of what is now Independence Pass on paths created partially by the Ute Indians and partially by wild animals. About halfway down they came upon the awesome sight we continue to see today: a misty gap in the mountains, and the shimmering still waters and marshy wetlands at the east end of the valley giving way to a strong northward bend in the river surrounded by a broad valley floor that was to become the present-day town of Aspen. Sheltering the valley to the north were the crimson rocks of Red Mountain, Smugglers Mountain, and Red Butte; protecting the valley in the south, an eternity of white-capped peaks starting with landmark Aspen Mountain and folding into some of the most picturesque mountain scenery in America—Maroon Bell, Pyramid Peak, and Mt. Sopris.

Word passed quickly about the phenomenal amount of silver buried under the peaks surrounding the Roaring Fork Valley. Almost instantly, more fortune hunters arrived and inched their way down the steep slopes to what promised to be one of the richest silver strikes in American history. Some came on foot. Some came on skis.

The wilderness was not without perilous risks. Indian raids and the harsh realities of high-altitude living were constant threats, as were avalanches, forest fires, and mining accidents. All took a heavy toll. Nevertheless, the silver that had made men

THIS PAGE: *Time stands still for one of the many thriving silver mines that made Aspen the richest city in America's silver circuit.*

OPPOSITE: *Fashionable ladies and gentlemen at the railroad station of affluent Victorian Aspen.*

NO ADMITTANCE

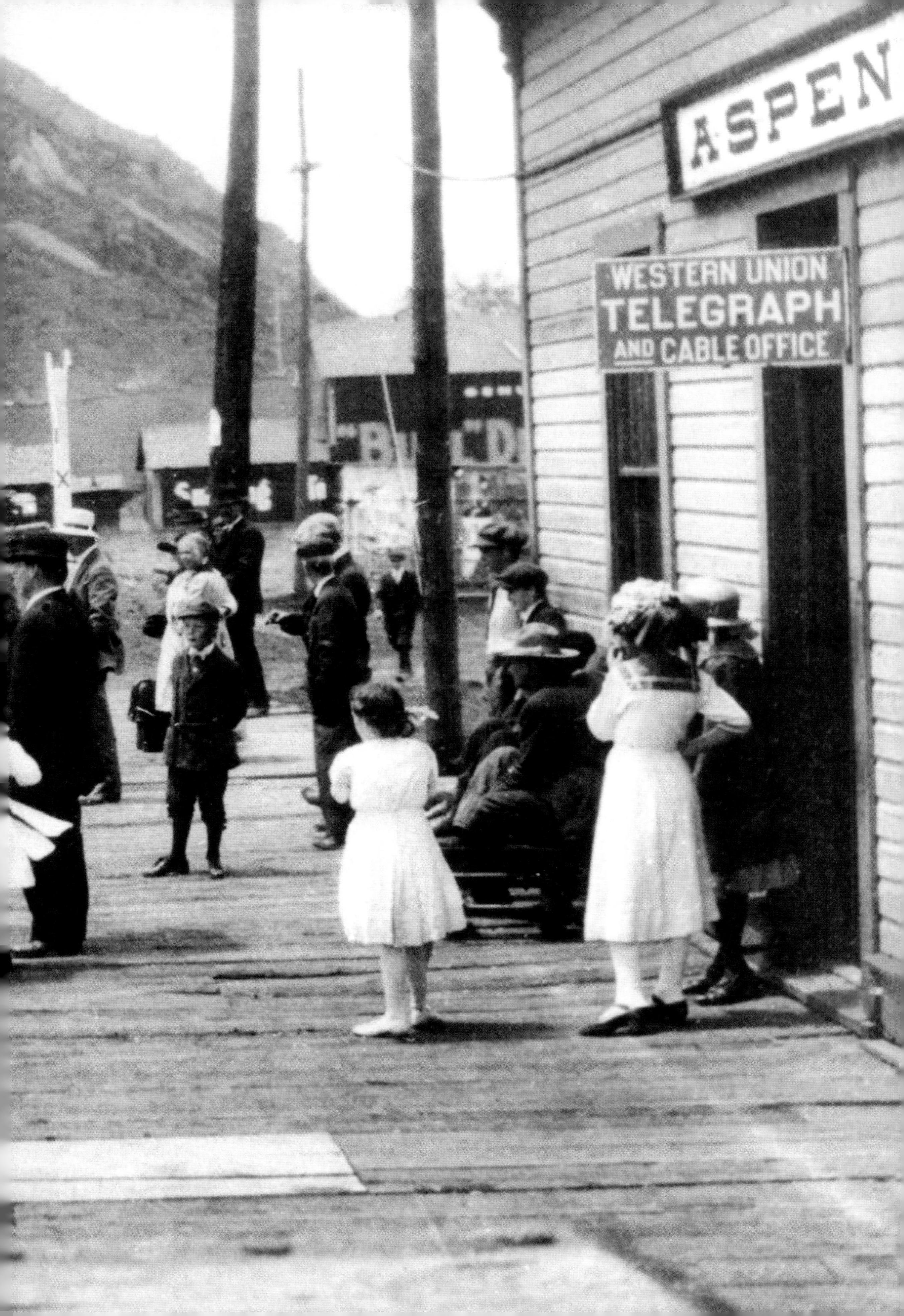
ASPEN
WESTERN UNION
TELEGRAPH
AND CABLE OFFICE

mighty rich in other places was a driving force for starting a serious new settlement in the wide valley twenty miles below Independence. The prospectors called their new settlement Ute City, as a sort of backhanded homage to the Ute Indians whose domain they had raided. Today, a ghost town is all that remains of the original Independence.

The isolated high-mountain plateau that would become Ute City had been a favorite winter refuge of the Ute Indians. For years they had raised horses and built birthing huts on the plateau and enjoyed the valley's hot springs. There is a clear account of at least one attempt by the Utes to resist invasion of their territory: The Meeker Massacre of 1879, which occurred when a settler tried to force the Utes to farm and plow the land. It resulted in an Ute ambush and the death of many settlers. As a consequence of the uprising, the Utes were banished to the reservation at Four Corners. In recent years, former U.S. ski champion and Colorado resident Suzy Chaffee and photographer-activist Connie Marlow have taken up the cause of these Native Americans.

As though afflicted with guilty consciences, the white settlers changed the name of Ute City to Aspen after the tall, white-barked tree found in the area. Within a year after the arrival of its first prospectors, Aspen became the richest silver town in the world. It boasted a mother vein 40 miles wide, something never heard of before. In 1894, as a further testament to the fabulous local mineral bounty, the Smuggler Mine produced the largest silver nugget ever found. The nugget (93 percent pure silver) was

LEFT TO RIGHT: *The Denver and Rio Grande was the first train to arrive in Aspen on November 1st, 1887; The first sundeck at the top of the chair-lift on Aspen Mountain after the Ajax mining claim; The Fred Glidden House, one of the landmark Victorian houses that became so popular with the younger generation, who arrived in 1952 at the start of Aspen's ski boom.*

pared down to 1,840 pounds so it could be carried from the shaft and paraded through the town of Aspen on an open, mule-drawn wagon like a magnificent trophy.

With all this hullabaloo, several East Coast entrepreneurs, as well as many Europeans, began to arrive in the remote little boomtown. Railroads, telephone lines, and a post office soon appeared, followed by saloons and a red-light district to accommodate the savvy prospectors and rowdy miners away from their wives and children. Soon after, the civilizing zeal of the Victorian Age took over and, with the arrival of lawyers, bankers, ministers, literary societies, temperance women, and respectable steep-roofed, porch-wrapped gingerbread houses, Aspen became the most glamorous enclave on the "Silver Circuit." It was the first city in the United States to be powered entirely by electricity.

With the help of promoters and exploiters such as Pennsylvania mining engineer B. Clark Wheeler, by 1883 about 700 people lived in Aspen. By 1889, the town had grown to 8,000. With the arrival of Jerome B. Wheeler (no kin to B. Clark Wheeler), the president of Macy's department store in New York and Aspen's first major benefactor, Aspen reached the apex of its style-conscious prosperity and Victorian vogue. Believing that a city with such rich fortunes should also assert itself as a community of substance and status, Wheeler proceeded to build the extravagant Wheeler Opera House. Gilt boxes, leather upholstered seats, domed ceilings studded with stars, and enormous chandeliers, combined with a grand opening night complete with scented satin

programs, attracted prominent people from coast to coast. "Sophistication was here early and that sophistication remains here to this day," says Wendy Morse, a Boston Brahmin who arrived in Aspen straight out of Yale, supporting his passion for skiing by washing dishes before founding Aspen's biggest real estate firm, Mason and Morse.

By 1892, Aspen's population had grown to 12,000. The town boasted three banks, ten churches, three sizable schools, a modern hospital, six newspapers, and a spate of first-class hotels. Foremost among these was the Hotel Jerome. To this day, the likes of Jack Nicholson, Italian ski legend Alberto Tomba, or Goldie Hawn's actress daughter Kate Hudson and her rock-star husband can be spotted walking through Hotel Jerome's lobby, quaffing an après-ski drink at the bar or having a quiet dinner next to the huge open fireplace decorated with mounted stag horns.

But alas, as so often happens in America's history, Aspen's overnight boom turned to bust. Fourteen years after the first prospectors bravely pioneered their way down from Independence Pass into the deserted high-altitude valley, the sparkle emanating from this little industrial and cultural experiment in the Rocky Mountains was suddenly dimmed. By the spring of 1893, the slowing of the U.S. economy began to be felt in the Rockies. The Sherman Silver Purchase Act of 1890 had originally doubled silver purchases, but also radically increased the amount of money in circulation. When President Grover Cleveland insisted that the

ABOVE: *Scandinavian sweaters were the rage with Aspen's early skiers in the 1950s. Aspen's Jim Ward, busy waxing his wooden skis, was no exception.*

OPPOSITE: *A still life of early skis, goggles, fur-trimmed hooded ski parka, lace-up boots, and snowshoes.*

Sherman Act threatened to undermine the U.S. Treasury's gold reserves, a special session of Congress was called to demonetize silver and shift the standard of currency to gold. In a last-ditch effort to promote silver, Aspenites sent a gem-encrusted silver statue of a woman in a chariot to the Chicago Exposition of 1893, but the gesture failed to rouse political support, and the Silver Queen, as she was called, mysteriously vanished.

In the economic crash that followed, mines ceased to operate, businesses closed, and fortunes were lost. Many of the lavish Victorian homes were boarded up; others were abandoned and eventually dismantled and used for firewood. Most of the silver barons became paupers overnight.

From the outset, Aspen has attracted hardy, self-reliant, and sophisticated people exhilarated by the drama of the mountains but also expecting to be rewarded for the risks they take in the wilderness. And though the population dwindled to only a little more than 600 during the sixty-year hiatus when Aspen faded from the national consciousness, enough families remained to keep the town alive. Though their wealth had vanished, the pioneering spirit of Aspen's people had not been broken. Their faith in this remote Rocky Mountain village encouraged Aspen to rise up again.

OPPOSITE: *Paul Hayes glides through the conifer forest on cross-country skis in the breathtaking Ashcroft Valley, where Aspen skiing was first pioneered in the 1930s.*

Ski & Snow

Winter is the season for which Aspen is best known. And winter never comes fast enough for those who want a deep snow base for November's ski-lift openings. The first snowfall is magic, sugarcoating the spruce trees, frosting the golden aspen boughs, and tracing the already stunning scenery with the illusion of a delicate, porcelain-like filigree. Later, the famous dry Colorado snows come drifting in at a steadier pace until finally winter hurls itself upon the ice-glazed high-altitude ponds and silent forsaken backcountry. Into this frozen world of forbidding distant peaks and ridges glistening in the bright morning sun come the masses of thrill and fun seekers who turn Aspen into an excitingly alive and sparkling hub.

The Aspen Skiing Company—the Rolls Royce of the ski industry—has never stopped revving its engines. After the lucrative years of the '60s, '70s and '80s, when Aspen was reputedly becoming cocky and unaffordable, Aspen Skiing raced to capture a new generation of cool, freestyle adventurers to maintain its title as king of American ski hills. The year 2001 saw many changes, all aiding and abetting a more youthful future for Aspen. First and foremost, Aspen Mountain dropped its notorious ban on snowboarding. Although snowboarding had been

ABOVE: *The dramatic zigzag spine of the ridge at Aspen Highlands, coated in its winter-white dazzle of snow and ice, is among the physical features of the region that give Aspen such a strong sense of place.*

OPPOSITE: *The apex of ski chic, circa 1957, skiwear mogul Klaus Obermeyer launches his Obermeyer Sports label from the top of Aspen Mountain with the supermodel of the day, Carmen dell'Orefice, at his side.*

LEFT TO RIGHT: *Skiers relish a glorious early morning in the spring of 1952 in the Little Nell area of Aspen Mountain, just above where today's five-star Little Nell Hotel reigns supreme as the hub of glamour; The latest ski complex to receive a major facelift is Aspen Highlands, where Gerald Hines is developing a whole new mountain base ski village with shops, restaurants, lodges, and condominiums; The first (and last) hot dog stand serving hungry Aspen skiers was called "Ski In." It was beloved by folks who had only one uphill means of transportation in those days: the famous Lift Number One.*

permitted at the other three mountains, a number of potential visitors thought that snowboarding was banned on all of Aspen's mountains. To prevent an entire generation of young customers from taking their ski dollars elsewhere, the anti-snowboarding wall came tumbling down to considerable fanfare. On April Fool's Day, 2002, the base of Aspen Mountain became a World Cup–style jamboree of manufacturers' tents, skiers, boarders, and spectators. The spring air was thick with the smell of suntan lotion and the energy of thousands of young people celebrating what was to become an annual Spring Jam. The ski complex also rejuvenated its image by encouraging skiers to "ride the tress" on the Back of Bell on Aspen Mountain, building a new "superpipe" for snowboarders at Buttermilk, and bringing a series of highly popular big-mountain "freeriding" (a form of extreme skiing) competitions to Highland Bowl and the Cirque at Snowmass.

True, there is no dearth of glossy, slim-hipped women flaunting the latest ski fashions and high-strung wheeler-dealers with cell phones glued to their ears even while riding the up-mountain gondola. Famous faces from politics and pop culture appear everywhere, and Aspen has a worldwide reputation as a winter perch of privilege and frenetic social buzz (an exclusive new private club on top of the mountain has reciprocity with the Corviglia Club in St. Moritz and the Eagle in Gstaad). Still, despite the glitz and ostentation, Aspen Mountain, with its gut-numbing chutes, wild backcountry, and incredibly challenging double-diamond plunges, continues to be the preferred

PAGE 37: *Film star Gary Cooper at the height of his popularity in the 1940s was the first Hollywood luminary to become an Aspen regular. He and his fashionable wife, Rocky, pausing here between runs at the Little Nell, were always turned out in the latest sportive garb and set the pace socially in their Red Mountain slopeside house.*

terrain of world-class skiers. Throughout the decades, they've all loved the place: Dick Durrance, Stein Eriksen, Tony Sailer, Anderl Molterer, Ingmar Steinmark, Jean-Claude Killy, Alberto Tomba, and many more.

Aspen has not always been the playground for such an impressive list of celebrities and skiing stars; in fact, in the annals of American skiing, it is often thought of as the "war baby." The three main forces that came together to bring about the financial rebirth of Aspen were all affected or brought about by World War II. Before the war, skiing was a rich man's sport, specific to the East Coast. The first push to turn Aspen into a resort came about in the '30s when former Connecticut congressman Ted Ryan, bobsledder Billy Fiske, and native Aspenite T.J. Flynn literally crash-landed their plane in the Roaring Fork Valley. They fell head-over-heels in love with the idea of establishing a ski area in the region above Aspen—specifically, in the splendid ghost-town valley of Ashcroft. They were so keen on the viability of Ashcroft as a future winter playground that they brought in the famous Swiss mountain engineer André Roch to plan the ski village and complex of lifts. The Colorado State Legislature even approved financial assistance for a tram to the top of Hayden Peak, which, according to Roch, held the greatest promise of becoming a varied and challenging ski complex. The newly formed ski corporation was called "Highland Bavaria," and Ted Ryan, the sociable and good-looking outdoorsman, was made its president and major stockholder.

"We called it Highland Bavaria because we all had such a great time with winter sports at Garmisch Partenkirchen and were stuffed with Bavarian delights in those days." From his East 57th Street office in New York, Ryan, along with his friend the late Benedict Quinn, gathered possible backers. "It was to be nothing but the best for us: Gordon B. Kaufman, who did the Jockey Club in Santa Anita, designed the lodge, and Walt Disney's number-one cartoonist Jimmy Bodrero did some of the Bavarian-style murals around the fabulous fireplace. We opened for Christmas 1936 with a memorable menu of consomme à la duchesse, salad epicurienne, turkey milanaise, Camembert, café à la viennoise, cigars and so forth."

World War II ended the fun. Billy Fiske, the gregarious, irrepressible leader of the group, joined Britain's Royal Air Force and was mortally wounded in the Battle of Britain. "With Billy dead, we all seemed to lose interest in recreational activities. People were saving steel for the war effort, so it didn't seem right to build chair-lifts." Instead, Ryan donated the use of the valley to the famed 10th Mountain Division (the same division that was first detached to combat Osama bin Laden in Afghanistan's mountain caves in fall 2001) for ski training. Just as Ted Ryan had hoped, many of these elite ski troops fell under the spell of the valley and the sport. Foremost among them was Friedl Pfeifer, an Austrian-born corporal who almost became the second Aspen ski catalyst to lose his life when his lung was shot out in the Italian mountain campaign. While he was training at Camp Hale, Colorado, Pfeifer spent every weekend on Ajax Mountain (today's Aspen Mountain), named after the Ajax Mine inside its slopes. Ajax reminded him so much of Austria's St. Anton that Pfeifer was convinced it could become the most sophisticated and all-around best ski resort in America. He, too, made contact with André Roch, who by that time was surveying the potential of the whole area with the Italian ski racer Gunther Langes. But Roch was underwhelmed by what he saw; he thought it ludicrous to imagine the run-down town of Aspen attracting socially prominent pacesetters who were accustomed to the pretty ski villages of Switzerland. Negative as Roch was, however, it was he who sparked the interest of native Aspenites and Colorado businessmen, inspiring them to

Making fashion statements and having a glorious time, a cosmopolitan crowd began to discover Aspen's many charms by the late 1940s and early '50s.

OPPOSITE: *Dapper in an ascot and sweater, Pete Seibert was crazy for Aspen's Victorian feel and halcyon days until he went on to start Colorado's other ski resort, Vail.*

THIS PAGE: *Flaunting the latest tailored look from the Alps in 1946, a radiant Georgette Taullier is flanked by two dynamos of American skiing: Friedl Pfeifer and Percy Rideout.*

inject new life into the forsaken silver center. With Frank and Fred Willoughby, Roch formed a fun-loving outing group called the Roaring Fork Winter Sports Club (later renamed the Aspen Ski Club). They started cutting the original 6,600-foot ski run down Aspen Mountain that was served by a leftover uphill mining contraption called the "boat tow." At day's end, everyone headed to the Hotel Jerome bar to drink "Aspen crud," a milkshake generously laced with brandy.

Aspen's success was ensured when Friedl Pfeifer teamed up with local investor Darcy Brown and Chicago industrialist Walter Paepke. The board chairman of the Container Corporation of America, Paepke, a third generation German-American, was deeply wounded by America's anti-German sentiment in 1945. Paepke began raising money among his industrialist friends for ski lifts, and in 1946 the Aspen Skiing Corporation was formed. No great fan of winter sports, Paepke envisioned Aspen as a summer cultural center and began to buy every piece of land in town. With his wife, Elizabeth, who hailed from a family of intellectuals, scholars, and musicians, he started the Aspen Music Festival and the Aspen Center for Humanistic Studies.

But the real turning point for Aspen came in 1950 when Aspen hosted the prestigious Federation Internationale de Ski (FIS) Championships. This event, more than any other, launched Aspen into the international orbit. To ready the mountain for this momentous occasion, skiing legend Dick Durrance was called in and made Vice-President of the Aspen Skiing Corporation. Durrance, America's first Olympic gold-medal winner, knew as much about skiing as anyone in the U.S. Major funding for the event came from Colorado's Coors Beer and the Colorado Power Company. The competition course received phenomenal praise from the international press. From then on, the attention of the ski world was focused on this unique little Rocky Mountain village and the town bathed in the glow of such glamorous post-war European visitors as Norway's blonde ski Adonis Stein Eriksen, France's world champion Henri Oreiller, Italy's Zeno Colo, and Austria's comely Dagmar Rom.

As proof that Aspen's pluses outnumber its minuses, most of the men responsible for its success have opted to remain in the valley. Those 10th Mountain Division men who carved out the slopes of Aspen after the war became local celebrities, among them the late architect Fritz Benedict and former editor in chief of *The Aspen Times* Bill Dunaway. The Aspen Skiing Company—as it was renamed in recent years—and its fortunes have indeed

OPPOSITE: *Elli of Aspen, as both she and her famous blue-painted boutique were known, was the main catalyst in developing a feminine Aspen style with a decidedly alpine flavor. Elli, who was on the Austrian ski team, came to Aspen as the wife of Swiss ski champion Fred Iselin. When Fred became Friedl Pfeifer's co-director of Aspen's ski school in 1954, she opened her shop and began to design her own ski outfits. They sold like hotcakes.*

PAGES 42-43: *Santa's little canine helper trudges through the fresh-fallen champagne powder at family-oriented Snowmass, which comes into its own at Christmas; Snowmobiles zip down the back of Aspen Mountain during the adrenaline-charged X Games.*

been as unique and quirky as the town it dominates. Once upon a time, the men behind it were just a bunch of ski buffs who fell in love with the sporting possibilities of this picturesque but economically dormant mining town; today, industry analysts estimate the value of the privately owned company at more than $200 million. Flushed with Star Wars dollars, Twentieth-Century Fox acquired it in the '70s and many of the studio's top brass took up residence in the mountains. The Aspen Skiing Company is now part of the vast Crown family empire, spearheaded by General Dynamics of Chicago. These days, Lester Crown, the popular patriarch of the clan, and several younger members live either part-time or full-time in the Roaring Fork Valley.

Nowhere is Aspen's original spirit more evident than in the annual crack-of-dawn start for America's Uphill, when hundreds of skiers, snowshoers, and runners plod uphill from the town base at Little Nell to the top of Aspen Mountain. This is no small feat, for Aspen Mountain is deceptively enormous, with intricate, diabolically demanding chutes and acres of magnificent open vistas. Even super-jock skiers on the latest short skis sometimes vanish for entire exhilarating days. The several mountain restaurants and infinite skiing pleasures that make up Aspen Mountain cannot be fathomed from below. Up in the remote empyrean lies the secret of Aspen's rapture and grandeur. For mile after mile, shining glaciers and velvet white snowfields ripple over the ridges as the vast silent spectacle of Maroon Bell, Castle, Cathedral, and Pyramid peaks rim the distance. Here, crack skiers thrill to some of the most infamous ski runs in North America, such as Elevator Shaft, which one annual pilgrim from Hawaii

ABOVE: *The Aspen ski bum is legend and he is alive and well. Here a British trio of classic ski bums from the 1980s who work as silver service waiters by night and hit the ski lifts all day. Sporting the mirrored specs of the day: Dominic Sanchez, Nick Malatet-Lee-Clarke, and Roland Topfi.*

OPPOSITE: *Airborne over Aspen, popular American champion Phil Mahre wows them all as he speeds down some gut-numbing terrain.*

describes as a sensation resembling "dropping down an open pit, descending into the depths of oblivion."

Even at the summit, Aspen Mountain accommodates the glamour crowd. Both the Sundeck and the new private Mountain Club welcome skiers with cozy seating arranged around huge atmospheric fireplaces. Shrines to Marilyn Monroe, Jerry Garcia, and Jimi Hendrix placed among the Aspen trees mark the path to Bonnie's, one of the most desirable places to be for lunch. Bonnie's sun-splashed terrace is the place to check out who else is in town, while refueling on weisswurst and sauerkraut, German dumpling soup, white wine, and fabulous trifle and strudel first made famous by the restaurant's original owner (and former German ski champion), the late Gretl Uhl. At the center of Bonnie's lunchtime social badinage is arguably Aspen's most popular bachelor: oil man Jack Crawford from Newport Beach, California. He has earned oodles of friends over the years by throwing an annual mountaintop bikini party.

Over at Aspen Highlands, however, one encounters a different set. Long favored by local elite skiers such as Chris Davenport, the world-renowned adventure skier, and Chris Klug, superstar Aspen snowboarder and 2002 Olympic-medal winner, the atmosphere at Highlands is all outdoors anticipation. Perhaps harking back to the old Highlands poster depicting Dick Durrance in mid-turn with the tag line "Lunch is for Sissies," there's no lingering around the fireplace in the lodge at the base of Highlands; here there's only energetic, red-cheeked young men and women eager to get back on the slopes. With the recent opening of the challenging Highland Bowl, many consider Highlands the ultimate in in-bounds backcountry experience. "It's just like off-piste, except it is legal," quips Billy O'Donnell, another extreme competitor. "There are no sounds, no people, no tracks." Aspen Highlands' popularity with locals originally sprang from a lower-cost season pass (which still exists) and is fueled today by new high-speed lifts that allow for rapid-fire laps in Steeplechase, west-facing runs such as Deception, and its unparalleled crown jewel, Highland Bowl. Indeed, the hike into the 12,382-foot bowl and the well-earned trip down have become required parts of the Aspen experience, at least for those with the requisite lung capacity and skiing or snowboarding skills.

Highlands has always been different. Founded in the '50s by former New Englander "Whip" Jones, Highlands served up a heady mix of derring-do, defiance, and superb skiing, all the while thumbing its nose at the Aspen Skiing Corporation with both humor and resolve. Jones bequeathed the mountain to his alma mater, Harvard University, which subsequently sold the property to developer Gerald Hines of Houston & London in 1993. Hines hooked up with the Aspen Skiing Company, which now operates the mountain, leaving Hines to concentrate on developing real estate. But the real secret of skiing the Highlands has been overshadowed by the thrill of Highland Bowl. The 30-minute slog up the 12,382 feet of Highland Peak may be a fashionable pastime for the real athletes, but it's entirely worth the trek simply for the rolling panorama of Colorado to which it leads.

For those who have been away from Aspen for a while, the new base village at Highlands is quite a surprise. After five years of securing the necessary approvals and several more of construction, it finally opened in 2001—but not without controversy. There are those who miss the decrepit '60s-style base lodge and the old bar with its carved graffiti, steamed-up windows, and authentic grunge feel. People complain about the seven-million-dollar homes and the Ritz-Carlton Club, a collection of time-share apartments that cost up to $250,000 for 28 days a year. Hines commissioned Robert A. M. Stern, dean of architecture at Yale University, to create a mountain village inspired by the Old Faithful Inn at Yellowstone and the Ahwahnee Hotel at Yosemite National Park, with, in Hines' words, the kind of "buildings that don't shrink in grandly scaled settings." There are many new faces at Highlands, more than a few of whom used to be regulars on Aspen Mountain. An old wooden ski patrol shack has been transformed into a terraced on-slope bistro called Cloud Nine, the type of spot that, in the old days, was found only in Europe. Despite this apparent gentrification, some relics of the old Highlands have been preserved, such as the handmade wooden trail signs, and "Freestyle Fridays" that still go off above the Merry-Go-Round restaurant. There are also subsidized condos or "affordable housing" to ensure the community will continue to be enlivened by young visitors as well as locals. "Let Gucci and Bulgari glitter in Aspen, three miles away.

PAGE 46: *In the high mountain valley, autumn's changing foliage is magically reflected in Hallam Lake. Unlike New England, Aspen's leaves never turn red.*

OPPOSITE: *The last day of skiing before the lifts close in mid-April culminates in Spring Fling, an afternoon of live rock music at the base of Aspen Mountain that then moves on to nearby Ajax Tavern.*

We're the trailhead to a glorious outdoors," maintains Georgia Hanson, retail manager for the Hines Development. Dave Durrance, Dick Durrance's son and owner of the ski shop at the Highlands, adds: "The New Highlands is like a new pair of jeans. It will only improve with use."

Across Maroon Creek is Aspen's real hometown hill, Buttermilk Mountain. Visitors tend to bring their children to the Buttermilk Ski School, perceiving it to be a mountain for kids and beginners, but Buttermilk is the mountain of choice for many true Aspenites. On any weekday morning, local mothers, doctors, artists, realtors, and carpenters who have pried themselves loose from a busy workday can be seen out on the slopes taking advantage of some irresistible morning powder. They zip happily down the Tiehack side, where there is never a lift line, performing their "daily constitutional"—a bottom-to-top workout on cross-country gear, snowshoes, or skis. Snowboarders and freestyle skiers hang out at Buttermilk to try out the kind of stunts that would get them booted off the other slopes.

Finally, there is Snowmass, a gigantic entity in its own right and the home of the Big Burn, a gladed glory half a mile wide and two miles long and famous for its deep powder, and the sensational Powder Horn with its 3,000 foot descent. Snowmass—a mountain resort and Aspen's fourth ski area was carved out in 1959 by one-time aviator, ski racer, art collector, cattleman, and Los Angeles land developer William Janss—has always had a familial feel to it, with the condominiums and slope-side chalets occupied by families who ski out of their homes right onto the beautifully groomed fairways. Here is one of Aspen's most demanding and discipline-requiring getaways: the backcountry hut-to-hut exploration of the original 10th Mountain Division hut system, accessible only on skis. This fabulous mountain experience, modeled on the French-Swiss Haute Route through the Alps, is the realization of Fritz Benedict's dream of a windswept wild trail system connecting Aspen with Colorado's other mega-resort, Vail.

Addicts who pour in from five continents agree: Aspen is the consummate ski resort. The mountains are so good, the downhill runs so satisfying to skier and snowboarder, beginner and expert, that they continue to draw true winter skiing fanatics despite the glamorous social scene. No matter what else happens in Aspen, the sporting American winter will always be among its biggest attractions.

OPPOSITE: *Ideal conditions, ideal terrain. From the top, among the undulating contours of the mountain, the possibilities are endless.*

A Stylish Little Town

ABOVE *Well-known sports journalists George Bouer and John Fry quaff their drinks in the bar of the Little Nell Hotel before they head off to a serious black-tie dinner.*

OPPOSITE: *During the Christmas season, Aspen's signature iron lampposts are festooned with 315 wreaths, pine boughs and twinkling lights. Horse-drawn sleighs whisk the likes of printing-press heir Thorne Donnelly and his wife, Trish, through the atmospheric Victorian streets.*

PAGE 57: *A period postcard of the far-famed Jerome Hotel, for more than a century the unceasing heartbeat of Aspen's social scene. It looked like this briefly in the '40s during Aspen's rebirth as a ski resort when Bauhaus architect Herbert Bayer tried to revamp its original Victorian brick facade to make it more appealing to modern worldlings.*

Below the sports going on in the mountains lies the city of Aspen, a totally original town in both form and substance, part big-city savvy, part small-town grit. To be sure, Aspen is famous for its excesses: $40-million mountain-view mansions with a fireplace in every room and a Jacuzzi in every bathroom, and 44-acre ranches with private training ovals; glittering fundraisers that would eclipse any big-city charity ball with ex-presidents and movie stars galore; million-dollar house-warming parties with buckets of Beluga caviar and potatoes gaufrette with white truffles and carne cruda; Natalie Cole flown in for after-dinner songs. Yet for all its reputation for excess, Aspen is also a place where many people still appreciate understatement, simplicity, even frugality. After all, the place was popularized a half-century ago by the original slackers: East Coast, Ivy League trust-fund babies who came to ski. They became intoxicated with the quirky lifestyle in the middle of nowhere and, working as bartenders and waiters in the first restaurants, many bought land when no one else believed Aspen had a future. Similarly, today many professional couples in their thirties and forties who tool around Aspen in four-wheel drives, dropping off children at

school or hockey games, are proud of their handmade hideaways in the woods and their cleverly space-efficient architect-built homes on tiny trailer-park plots. As they shoulder their skis or settle onto their mountain bikes against the brilliant sunshine and blue sky, they smile about the fact that they are able to carve out a stylish, creatively satisfying, health-and-fitness oriented life in paradise—on a shoestring.

Ultimately, the town of Aspen is the locomotive that drives one of the most fascinating valleys on earth and strongly influences the economy and lifestyle of growing numbers of interesting communities along the Roaring Fork River. Because of this, it demands and receives terrific attention. With the attractive people on its streets, the rich variety of shops and world-class restaurants, the famous unique hotels, and, yes, even the astronomical prices commanded by its real estate, Aspen long ago entered the national consciousness. It has come to be associated with a certain eccentric elegance, roguish experimentation, and irreverent sportive chic that all add up to an eclectic mix of styles that fits with how people want to live today.

"Aspen has become a brand," says Janet O'Grady, editor in chief of *Aspen Magazine.* "It stands for a certain quality of life—a culture based on art and sport in a matchless mountain town. Aspen stands for fit, enlightened people who have dreams and figure out ways to get what they want—even if they sometimes have to bend the rules a bit." O'Grady herself is a model of the Aspen ideal she describes. Having come to Aspen with her husband initially for the skiing and culture, O'Grady has built up the Aspen enterprise in her smart, glossy magazine that captures the true pulse of valley.

Aspen has attained a certain trendsetting status in other areas as well. Some years ago an automobile model named "Aspen" became the biggest sales success in Dodge history. A steamy novel called *Aspen* sold two million copies and was later made into a TV mini-series. The mystique of the Aspen name has been bottled into a perfume and a soft drink. Now plans are underway to market the local drinking water under the label "Aspen."

History has granted Aspen buildings that create a mood all their own, where the dreams of the early min-

Hotel Jerom
Aspen, Colo

PAGES 58-59: *A caricature of the celebrated "who's who" and select seating order at the Caribou Club, the first elite private club to succeed in an American mountain resort.*

LEFT TO RIGHT: *A graceful sleigh glides past one of the stately Victorian mansions built by silver barons of the late 1800s and refurbished when the ski boom brought a whole new generation of wealthy Americans to Aspen in the '50s; The Parisian post-war vogue for fancy "headdress-only" costume parties came to Aspen in the '50s, adding fizz and fun to the aprés-ski frivolities; Celebrities and media began to trickle into town around this time. Avid skiers Lex Barker, Hollywood's Tarzan, and film goddess Lana Turner were welcomed to the 1953 Wintersköl by Lennie Woods at the mike.*

eral kings are played against the aspirations of contemporary culture. The ostentatious Victorian mansions, located mainly on the West End, reflect the early pioneers' fervent desire to bring the outside world into the Roaring Fork Valley. By imitating the look of cities in the eastern United States and Europe, these first families hoped to identify Aspen as a community of consequence. For Aspen's prominent citizens of the 1800s, the Victorian style represented stability. In these times, the West End was the most stylish part of town, with the biggest multi-gabled mansions bordering Hallam Lake—the area where today Leonard Lauder, David Koch and Jack Nicholson own properties. But the smaller Victorian cottages in Aspen's East End, which were mass-produced and once belonged to the workers in the mines, are also in great demand these days. Though luxurious condominiums along the burbling creek sell in the $1.5 million range, the East End is still where more of "working Aspen" lives.

One unchanged aspect of Aspen is its penchant for style and fun. Even in Victorian times, Aspen dandies, dudes, and laced-up ladies knew how to make the most of the sporting life. When the bicycle arrived in the late 1880s, it became an instant craze. Men in sporting blazers and women in bloomers raced along a quarter-mile bike track. There was a half-mile horseracing track in, one hundred covered stalls for horses, and lots of high betting. Greyhound races and fencing matches brought Austro-Hungarian nobles to town; the moneyed mineral kings

played polo. When the snows came, the pretty Victorian town turned into one giant Currier and Ives Christmas scene.

Thousands of skaters would take to the ice in town on frozen Hallam Lake, while up on the Roaring Fork, skaters would glide from Sparkey's cabin to what is now the North Star Preserve. Before Olins and Rossignols, Aspenites tooled around on wooden slats they called "Norwegian snow shoes." All through the town the music of sleigh bells could be heard as young and old joined the sleigh rides. As many as thirty people burrowed under great big buffalo hides as the sleighs headed out to frozen lakes where huge bonfires lit the festivities. Hot rum, spiked eggnog and spirited song would bring together miners, lumbermen, carpetbaggers and members of Society's "400" during a winter night's merriment.

The 1950 FSI championships really brought Aspen to life. Johnny Litchfield, one of the returning 10th Mountain Division Veterans, transformed Gallaghers's old saloon into a new hangout for visitors and locals alike. He called it the Red Onion, and to this day it remains a popular Western saloon-style watering hole. Litchfied was among the first to sport a look that to this day is classic casual Aspen—a Scandinavian sweater over jeans, and a kerchief tied inside the neck of a Brooks Brothers shirt, with a silver-buckled Western belt, and cowboy boots. The powerful Swiss Team right away took to having lunch at "Litchi's" Red Onion. In the evenings French ski champ Henri Oreiller, whom all the Americans called "O'Reilly," provided many

laughs as he teamed up on the piano with the Swiss team's harmonica-playing Billy Zaug.

News of the fabulous races (as well as goodwill, fun and sportsmanship) traveled around the world, bolstering Aspen's international image. At a time when America was just discovering the pleasures and amusements of winter, some of the European champions, such as Stein Eriksen, Tony Sailer (who later started Vail), and Zeno Colo, were living gods of winter. But after the 1950 downhill competition, many of the ski stars of the American team—Andrea Mead, Bill Lawrence (who became her husband), Steve Knowlton, and Gale Spence—made Aspen their home. Several Europeans, such as Norway's Eriksen and Switzerland's Fred Iselin, also returned to live and work in Aspen. Fred's fashionable wife, Elli, opened the first skiwear boutique. Within the next few years, a definite Aspen style emerged. German champion Klaus Obermeyer became America's leading skiwear and equipment mogul. It was he who brought the turtleneck to the slopes, invented the quilted down ski parka by cutting up his mother's old duvet, and later engineered the revolutionary dual-construction ski boot, pre-shaped ski gloves, mirror sunglasses, and first high-altitude sunscreen.

OPPOSITE: *With the new surge of merriment that accompanied the ski boom, the old Western-style watering hole that was Gallagher's Saloon during the mining era was converted into a chic new aprés-ski meeting place: Johnny Litchfield's Red Onion.*

THIS PAGE: *The grand old Jerome Hotel, built in 1889 by the retired president of Macy's department store, as it looks today. Always the epitome of the good life, it has been a hangout and a hideaway for the rich and famous from the time of John Wayne.*

Aspen was becoming a melting pot of "Rocky Mountain High" and pizzazz from the Alps, solid Eastern-educated sportsmen and Hollywood high glamour. Photographs of all the attractive men in Aspen began to circulate and soon beautiful young women, too, began arriving. Lana Turner and John Wayne hung out at the Jerome's J-Bar. After Gary Cooper bought one of Fritz Benedict's Red Mountain houses, Aspen's position as a chic winter getaway was secured.

"These were incredible people and they set the tone for Aspen's cosmopolitan flavor," recalls Aspen society doyenne Merrill Ford. Walter Paepke's wife, Elizabeth, and her friends, Fabi Benedict and Joella Bayer, the daughters of French poet Mina Loy, started a salon culture in Aspen, hosting lively soirees of wicked conversation and an eclectic range of special guests, from playwrights to movie stars, from senators to Elizabeth's brother Paul Nitze, then Secretary of the Navy.

As skiing steered Aspen toward rebirth, the charming Victorian houses appealed to a whole new generation that put enormous effort into preserving their homes' aesthetic integrity. With the skiers' dollars, a new Aspen gentrification

ABOVE *Encircled by the snow-streaked Colorado Rockies, Aspen's tiny airport is chock a block with the lavish private jets of the millionaires and billionaires who come to the little town to ski in winter and take in the cultural fare during summer.*

OPPOSITE: *Ready for a formal Aspen evening, his tux wrapped under a vintage raccoon coat, Art Pfister, rancher, war-hero, and the mastermind behind the prestigious Maroon Creek Golf Club, is one of Aspen's leading citizens.*

PRESENTING

THE LIONS OF ENTERTAINMEN BUSINESS, SPORTS & SOCIETY

Harley Baldwin, an Aspen resident of 25 years, is owner and oftentime host at the Caribou Club.

The Caribou is a private club for dinner and dancing that would not have worked a few years ago. Aspen

took place and houses that sold for a few thousand dollars in 1940 were worth a few million by the 1970s. Although Aspen's downtown core is small enough to be walkable, the place is officially designated "The City of Aspen." Latest government figures proclaim it the third wealthiest city in the United States per capita. While Aspen is a National Historic District, today its quick-pulsed ambiance is decidedly contemporary. Aesthetically, the blend of contrasting historic eras is startling, sometimes even out-and-out strange. Here, far away from the rest of civilization, is a fancy relic of the Victorian Age, which was itself a time of eclectic and eccentric design styles. The unusual architectural aggregate of Wild West facades, century-old gingerbread houses, red sandstone strongholds with neo-Gothic windows and Greek revival columns are interspersed with the occasional mall-style arcades featuring today's most famous designers. Chanel, Christian Dior, Gucci, Prada, Ralph Lauren, Baccarat, Brioni and Frette are next door to age-old eateries with names harking back to Aspen's mining days—Little Annie's, the Mother Lode, the Red Onion, and the Crystal Palace. These in turn are flanked by Tyrolian chalets with names like Wienerstube or Innsbruck Inn, echoing the alpine influence of the early days of skiing. An old-fashioned popcorn wagon, draft horses and buggies on Independence Square are juxtaposed against stretch limos, out of which step beautifully groomed women in lavish fur coats, holding on to the leashes of several thoroughbred dogs.

Some of the real trendsetters today are Aspen's stellar chefs. Charles Dale, the son of a diplomat and close friend of Prince Albert of Monaco, trained in the south of France and in New York with Jean-George Vongerichten and Daniel Boulud. His two restaurants, the five-star Renaissance and the less formal Rustique, are where some of Aspen's most stylish people congregate for dinner. The Renaissance is famous for its five-course or—if you can go the distance—nine-course tasting menus.

Todd English serves a whiff of Mediterranean at Olives, where basketball great Michael Jordan or actresses Sally Field and Kate Hudson might be spotted at one of the banquettes around the holidays. A favorite of the jeans and leather-jacket aprés-ski crowd, Olives specializes in "layers of flavors," such as roast loin of rabbit glazed with balsamic vinegar over polenta and radicchio. The sesame-seared tuna at Little Nell's Montana is a favorite of year-round Aspenites. The Ute City

PAGES 66-67: *Aspen is a place where individuality and enterprising spirit are appreciated. Two unimpeachable Aspen originals are former New Yorkers Harley Baldwin and "Curious George" Lapin.*

LEFT: *Baldwin is social arbiter and master of ceremonies at the private Caribou Club.*

RIGHT: *Lapin, an Old Snowmass rancher, presides over one of the most unusual shops in town—a fascinating showcase for authentic Wild West memorabilia.*

OPPOSITE: *Handsome bronze stags greet guests at the lovely entrance and inner courtyard of Aspen's newest luxury hotel, the St. Regis, built on the most hotly contested piece of real estate in American history.*

Known as the "Gods of Winter," these handsome European ski champions were surrounded by women and admired by men when they made the scene in Aspen.

THIS PAGE: *The phenomenal Austrian champion Toni Sailer, whose incredible ski career included three Olympic gold medals and whose charisma on the mountain, as well as après-ski, earned him the jovial title "Honorary Sheriff of Aspen."*

OPPOSITE: *Norwegian Stein Eriksen arriving for the 1950 FIS competition in Aspen gave every indication of what was to follow: a gold and silver medal in the 1952 Olympic Games in Oslo, three gold medals in the 1954 FIS in Sweden.*

s 1957

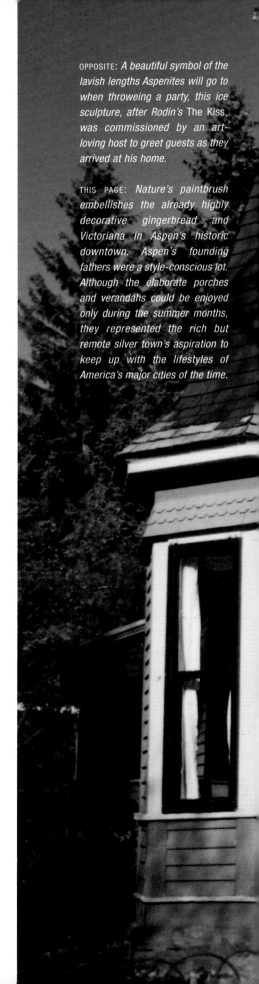

Bar & Grill used to be a bank and still has the old steel safe as part of its atmospheric nineteenth-century décor. It's a marvelous bistro and aprés-ski bar scene. There is no end to the dizzying variety of taste treats for sophisticated palates, from the brie-and-mango quesadillas and chili-rubbed ribeye at Blue Maize, a casual local favorite, to the more dressy people-watching places such as the Hotel Jerome's Century Room or Willow Creek at the Ritz Carlton Club at Aspen Highlands.

Aprés-ski has a life of its own in Aspen; for some it begins after their last run at 3:30 p.m. and goes on until dawn. It is at the end of the ski day that Aspen most palpably throbs with life. Skiers come off the mountain and land at the Ajax Tavern, swapping tall tales of the day's adventures in deep snow and bragging of cliff jumping courage. The Greenhouse at The Little Nell is a real see-and-be-seen scene, where cosmopolitan singles make new friends or meet old pals, Whoopie Goldberg cracks jokes among friends, and Clint Eastwood takes it easy by the bar. The J-Bar is still the occasional hangout of Jack Nicholson, while St. Regis's Lobby Lounge, with its welcoming fireplace and Pendelton blanket–draped leather chairs is one of the nicest ways to warm up during the wild winter twilight. At Rande Gerber's Whisky Rocks, one might see monologist Spalding Gray doing a solo

number in the center of the floor with his young baby strapped to his chest. Though Aspen's aprés-ski is democratic, unrelenting, and uninhibited, it goes private at the Caribou Club, which has been likened to Annabel's in London or Castel's in Paris. Rich with Hollywood glamour and the star power of Kevin Costner, Don Johnson, Sean Connery, Bruce Willis, Sylvester Stallone, Milla Jovovich and Steve Martin, the antler-chaired and -chandaliered Caribou Club is particularly festive during New Year's week and its secret "in season" (Thanksgiving through the early days of December).

Shopping Aspen's serendipitous world can be a sport as exhilarating as skiing its slopes. When the snow falls softly and the old Victorian lamps light the town's brick-paved streets, Aspen becomes a winter garden of earthly delights. Rare crafts by Zuni, Navajo, and Arctic artists compete for attention with fanciful sweaters or novel leather-and-loden hunting clothes. A wonderland of ski gear and mountain wear is on display at Gorsuch, one of the most lavish stores in town, and sturdy staples are easily found at Roots and Aspen Outfitters. Chocolate makers, cookie bakers and charcuteries like Les Chefs d'Aspen and the Rocky Mountain Chocolate Factory spew appetizing aromas into the streets outside. Many of the most original shops in Aspen were started by people who came to ski but fell in love with the town during the summer season when the atmosphere is more intellectual and artsy. Perhaps the most extraordinary example of this is The Explore Bookshop, the brainchild of Katharine Thalberg, a former television writer and daughter of 1930s Hollywood legend Irving Thalberg and Norma Shearer. Another Aspen original is the stylish overload, the sometimes outright-silliness at Amen Wardy's store. This shop-owner has stacked the walls with anything but ordinary gifts, from gourmet Texas corn relish to Kenyan leopard bowls, "Wild West" Christmas ornaments to white-chocolate and praline "reindeer food." Despite his elegant taste in antiques, crystal, silver and porcelain, in the best Aspen tradition, Wardy doesn't take himself too seriously. Exemplifying the spirit of Aspen, he marches about town with his five grand poodles and two Great Pyrenees, content in his achievement of blending humor with the art of living well.

OPPOSITE: *Shopping Aspen's eclectic streets is a serendipitous pleasure. Old-fashioned Western eateries, chocolate makers and cookie bakers fill the nippy winter air with their tempting fragrances. Colorado craftsmen—potters, weavers, leather workers—compete with designer boutiques.*

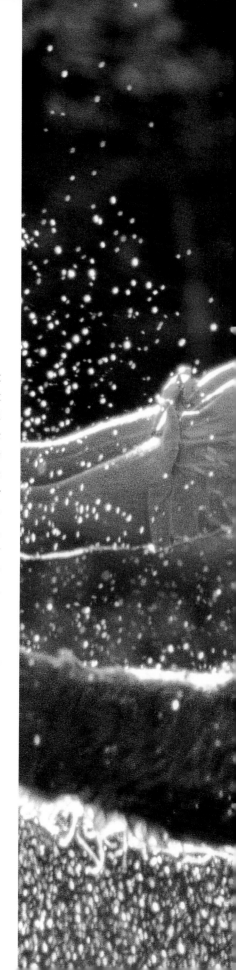

The Great Outdoors

The notion of wilderness suggests man's absence. It is a concept that resides somewhere in the recesses of the mind from where it generates a comforting wellspring of consistency, normalcy, and permanence. Wilderness in a rapidly changing world remains one of the last great constants, a place where man can mark his life against the perfection of nature. In Aspen, wilderness is the alpine majesty that surrounds the Roaring Fork Valley. There is no better place to contemplate man's place in the universe than tucked into a warm sleeping bag looking out on one of the most photographed nature sanctuaries in the lower 48 states. With the Hunter Fryingpan Wilderness bordering Aspen to the east and Collegiate Peaks and Maroon Bell–Snowmass wilderness areas to the south and west, the fundamental values of nature are visible everywhere.

When the high country reaches its midsummer peak, flowers of every description pattern Aspen's meadows. The Colorado Blue Columbine, discovered by Edwin James in 1820 and protected by law in 1825, was decreed the state flower in 1899. Native Americans used a tea made of the Columbine's seeds to cure headaches and fever. The Pasqueflower is one of the first unusual blooms to push through the icy earth in early spring, ushering in a welcome change to the seasons with its subtle violet beauty. Elusive and rare, the Pasqueflower appears in the wet valley floors amid dense woodlands. As the False Hellebore, or Skunk Cabbage, thrusts upward in bold, colorful shoots only inches from the retreating snowpack, the wildflower spectacle moves slowly into the high mountain valley. Mountain Lady's Slipper, Monkshood, Lupine, Aster, Fireweed, and King's Crown all follow the disappearing snow line, streaking the ground with bright pinks, brilliant

OPPOSITE: *Peter Hutter, a supremely skilled Aspen climber, doing his thing on a sheer vertical drop on a granite mountain wall near Independence Pass.*

THIS PAGE: *A plunge as clean, clear and cooling as a mountain pond in mid-July, taken by Peter Smith and his golden retriever Sir Winston at Crystal Lake.*

Sports fishermen from four continents come to Aspen in quest of the famous Rocky Mountain trout, subject of Richard Brautigan's cult book *Fly-Fishing in America*. Today the fish are ferociously watched over by such guardians of the wilderness as A.C.E.S. (Aspen Center of Environmental Studies) at Hallam Lake.

blues, and every variety of yellow and white blooms. July's Indian Paintbrush, named for its paintbrush-like red, pink, and yellow flowers, is one of the best-known Rocky Mountain wildflowers and carpets the lovely green heights by July. Delicate Alpine Forget-Me-Nots crouch low in the tundra, contrasting with the tall Green Gentian, while Miner's Candle bursts with blossoms in forest glades. Colorado's wildflowers describe the beauty of nature's vibrant handiwork and they are highly valued as part of the natural landscape. Author Paul Anderson, an expert on the flora, fauna, and ecosystems of the White River National Forest, describes the infinite variety of vegetation in the western part of the state. Colorado's Recreation Land Preservation Act, passed in 1971, has made it a crime to "willfully cut down, break or otherwise destroy any living tree, shrubbery, wildflower or natural flora." The maximum fine is $500.

Aspen takes its natural beauty as seriously as its sport, and wilderness preservation (which makes up roughly two percent of the landmass of the lower 48 states) is supported by its advocates with an almost religious fervor. At least thirty trails in the Aspen-Snowmass area belong to the White River National Forest and are maintained by the U.S. Forest Service. Topographic maps give a clear picture of the steepness and contour of the routes as well as the time and stamina required by hikers who take them on. The Ashcroft area offers classes in wilderness skills, astronomy, and mountain-plant identification. Rock climbing and mountaineering, especially around the steep Independence Pass, can be arranged through Aspen Alpine Guides at Aspen Expeditions.

The wealth of wild beauty and fascinating ecosystems that wrap a frontier of unspoiled nature around Aspen makes the resort a pivotal point for access to rushing trout streams and tranquil high-altitude lakes. In the Frying Pan River fishermen in hip waders whip their fly-fishing rods. On the Roaring Fork, whitewater rafters speed through foamy rapids while kayakers paddle through the eddies. Mountain bikers traverse groves in Woody Creek and head for rugged paths along the high ridges of timberline.

The favorite saying in Aspen goes like this: "I came for the winter but I stayed because of the summers." As one ski instructor, an Australian professional big mountain competitor who has skied Chamonix, Mt. Kilimanjaro, and the Himalayas, puts it, "It was the snow that brought me here—but where else could you wake up on a beautiful summer morning, stare simultaneously at your mountain bike, kayak, para-glider, and hiking boots, and have to make the tough decision of how you're going to spend the day?"

PAGES 82-83: *The lure of the winter-white wilderness is all around Aspen.*

LEFT: *A frozen glade of Aspen trees—their tall white trunks characteristically bearing black markings that resemble mystical eyes—lead down into the stark, peaceful world of silent nature around Conundrum Creek.*

RIGHT: *A horse-drawn sleigh dashes into the endless forest of spruce and fir, weighted with fresh-falling snow, for a romantic escape into the idyllic backcountry around the ghost town of Ashcroft.*

OPPOSITE: *In autumn, when the wind rustles through the aspen trees turned gold, Maroon Creek Road becomes a favorite gateway for hikers, mountain bikers, and horseback riders to the matchless mountain scenery of Maroon Bell and the jagged, snow-frosted contours of Pyramid Peak.*

Aspen Ideas & Ideals

The creation of Aspen as a European-style culture center in a lovely natural setting in the American West—a sort of Salzburg, Montreux, Avignon and San Sebastian rolled into one—was the accomplishment of a Chicago couple, Walter and Elizabeth Paepke. Today's Aspen Institute, Aspen Music Festival, Aspen International Design Conference, Aspen Physics Center, Aspen Film Fest, Aspen Food & Wine Classic, Aspen–Santa Fe Ballet and Jazz Aspen all directly or indirectly trace their origins to what has come to be known as "The Aspen Idea." Today, the Aspen summer thrives as a coming-together of some of the biggest talents and most powerful men and women from around the world because of its reputation as a place conducive to learning that encourages freedom of self-expression. The brainchild of businessman Paepke, "The Aspen Idea" infused the town with its intellectual identity and established it as a community that champions intellectual creativity.

Paepke was a man of unusual acumen and vision, as he proved when he turned his father's modest holdings into the nation's largest packaging company, Container Corporation of America. Besides being an industrialist, Paepke was also an ideologue. He had long been involved in the intellectual and cultural

ABOVE: *Art and music, academicians and aesthetes descended upon Aspen in the 1950s and brought about the town's renaissance as a virtual university in the mountains. This work of art comments on Aspen's cultural legacy.*

OPPOSITE: *The Aspen Music Festival tent has become a real scene. This 1988 hand-colored etching by Adair Peck depicts a typical summer afternoon's collection of culture vultures who start reading and picnicking on the lawn by mid-afternoon to secure a free spot in which to listen to the world-class musicians playing inside the gigantic, gently flapping canvas.*

Legendary humanitarian Dr.
Albert Schweitzer made his one
and only journey to America
from his French West African
hospital in 1949. His visit drew
the world's attention to the tiny
Rocky Mountain town.

life of Chicago and was deeply influenced by the Greek ideal of the fulfilled life: a combination of work, play, and educational leisure. In the slumbering little town of Aspen, Paepke saw the sublime venue for a utopia where the Socratic model of the perfect life might become a reality through a combination of art, music, literature, debate, and sport. He had hoped to make Aspen into an "Athens of the West," a marriage of culture and commerce. This philosophical underpinning of Aspen's economic renaissance in the early 1950s was the essence of "The Aspen Idea." Originally Paepke had a romantic vision of improving Aspen through use of its natural resources: Aspen wood for crafts that could be sold; native silver for jewelry; clothes out of wool from Aspen's sheep; and cheese and butter from the cattle. But Paepke's moneyed associates convinced him that Aspen's greatest resource was snow. Although the town strayed from Paepke's idealistic vision when Aspen became a world-class ski resort with a private jet airport and a billion-dollar real estate industry, the cerebral influence of "The Aspen Idea" has remained powerful enough to distinctly color the Aspen experience. There is no other mountain town in the world where so much effort and so many events are devoted to improving the mind and body, the quality of life, and the state of the world.

The Aspen Company, which by 1950 had become The Aspen Institute of the Humanities, shared many investors with The Aspen Skiing Corporation. Its purpose was to provide "a community of peace" in the Platonic sense where one "can earn a living and profit by healthy physical recreation, with facilities at hand for the enjoyment of art, music and recreation." When Paepke first brought his vision to Aspen's citizenry in the Pitkin County Courthouse, his suggestions for "the good life" and attracting "the best people" were not well received. After all, who was this stranger telling Aspen how to live? Furthermore, many locals still hoped for the return of mining, and they suspected that Paepke was a speculator and resented his interference. Nevertheless, there were some who believed that Paepke's seemingly far-fetched vision might have far-reaching possibilities.

One of Paepke's first steps was to bring Herbert Bayer to Aspen. Bayer, a German architect and artist, immigrated to the United States just before the war. Already well known

for his work with Laszlo Moholy-Nagy at the Art Institute of Chicago, Bayer had been retained by Paepke's Container Corporation in the early forties to produce a number of riveting designs for the company's cutting edge advertisements. The memorable ad campaign was themed "Great Ideas of Western Man" and each advertisement combined artwork by Miró, Magritte, or Ben Shawn with words by Aristotle, Dante, or John Locke. The collection is now the property of the Smithsonian.

Bayer soon became the artistic force behind transforming the mountain village of Aspen into a cultural retreat. Bayer's mission was to articulate architecturally and visually what "The Aspen Idea" was all about. In his mind, the idea relied on the synergy of dedicated people coming together with forward-thinking concepts. For Bayer, nothing defined this better than the ideals and principles of the Bauhaus, where he had been both student and master during the 1920s. In planning the physical layout of what was to become the Aspen Institute campus, Bayer applied the Bauhaus credo—integration of art and design with the larger sphere, practiced without hierarchy separating artist and craftsman—to its fullest realization. His buildings, sculpture, murals, textiles, graphics, earthworks, and today's popular "marble garden" all came together to form a cohesive whole. These functional and minimal geometric volumes of the understated Bauhaus aesthetic—which wholly contrasted with Victorian Aspen—have held up very well. They continue to set a tranquil, modern atmosphere for much of Aspen's ambitious creative activity.

Walter Paepke, who died in 1960 at the age of sixty-three, always had maintained close ties to Chicago's intellectual nucleus, the University of Chicago. In the late forties, the University of Chicago was a font of exciting philosophic controversy. In 1948, with two of the University of Chicago's most prominent intellectuals, Robert M. Hutchins and Mortimer Adler, Paepke conceived a

GOETHE
Bicentennial Convocation and Music Festival

Souvenir Program
$1.50

Aspen, Colorado, U.S.A. June 27 - July 16, 1949

dramatically idealistic plan: to bring together the world's intellectual leaders for a conference promoting humanistic ideals. In the culturally adrift world that was so politically tense after the inhumanities of World War II, "humanism" was a meaningful word. The conference Paepke envisioned would promote humanism while celebrating the bicentennial of the German poet Goethe's birth.

The organization's brightest idea was to hold the event not in urban Chicago, but rather to try and lure the cognoscenti to Aspen, a pastoral setting far from the distractions of the city. The obvious first choice for a site was the old Wheeler Opera House, which had been gutted by a fire in 1912 and was still charred. Bayer began to restore it, but a much more exciting plan was underfoot: the building of a giant amphitheater on Paepke's aspen-gladed property. Its designer was the famous Finnish architect Eero Saarinen and the theater was to be covered by canvas with sides that

ABOVE & OPPOSITE: *Held in the bleak shadow of World War II with its evils of totalitarianism and mechanization, the 3-week Goethe Bicentennial Festival in 1949 put Aspen on the map as a nascent culture center. Celebrating the ideals of two admired humanists—German poet, novelist and dramatist Goethe (1749-1832) and French clergyman, music scholar, philosopher, and physician Dr. Albert Schweitzer (1875-1965)—the event was the phenomenally ambitious undertaking of Walter Paepke. It brought poets, playwrights, and musicians of international renown to Aspen.*

Great Ideas of Western Man
. . ONE OF A SERIES

Jane Addams
on the basis of civilization

Civilization

is a method

of living,

an attitude

of equal

respect

for all men.

(Speech, Honolulu, 1933)

Container Corporation of America

Artist: George Giusti

PAGE 98: *From the "Great Ideas of Western Man" series of advertisements for Walter Paepke's Chicago-based Container Corporation of America. Arresting graphics by the likes of Magritte and Ben Shawn combined with thoughts by famous writers and thinkers extolled the idealistic mid-century values underpinning cultural Aspen.*

PAGE 99: *This fabulous al fresco lunch celebrating the 50th anniversary of the International Design Conference in Aspen (IDCA) in August 2001, seated 400 design insiders at tables snaking around the Aspen Institute grounds. Encouraging provocative dialogue in all areas of design worldwide, the eating engagement was itself a design by French artist Lucy Orta, entitled 70 x 7.*

could open to allow in the sun but close in case of rain. It would hover over an audience of 2,000 people and house a major orchestra. The orchestra chosen was the Minneapolis Symphony under Dmitri Mitropoulos, and other world-famous musical artists were invited to perform as well. However, as it was so soon after World War II, Arthur Rubinstein, Gregor Piatigorski, Leonard Bernstein, and Nathan Milstein were not easily convinced that they wanted to participate in a festival celebrating a German. But Paepke, as always, was persuasive, and they agreed to attend. For the intellectual aspects of the Bicentennial, the speakers were American playwright Thornton Wilder and Spanish philosopher Ortega y Gasset. Ultimately, the legendary humanitarian Albert Schweitzer, who made his one and only trip to the United States for Paepke's conference, drew the world's attention to little Aspen. The celebration turned out to be an event of epic proportions and enduring results. Hundreds of people streamed through the mountains in June 1949 to gather under Saarinen's sleek tent with its unusual slope and airy ambience. Critics and concert-goers were enthralled. So inspired were the festival's thinkers and performers that their three-week philosophizing carried over to conversations at garden parties and on mountain hikes. And so the Aspen Institute and Aspen Music Festival were both launched.

Indeed, with all the famed natural wonders that draw crowds into Aspen, one of the most fascinating aspects is the intellectual contributions that have come out of the legendary Aspen Institute. After more than fifty years, the Aspen Institute has grown into a

LEFT TO RIGHT: *In the 1960s contemporary art came to Aspen in a big way. Roy Liechtenstein was in town for the important Pop Art exhibit at the Aspen Institute in 1967; At the 2000 Aspen Institute Conference, World Bank president Wolfenson welcomes a worldwide who's who from business, politics, science, and the arts for a lively series of parties and seminars; New York artist Claes Oldenburg came for the 1967 Pop Art exhibit and, despite a fear of towering mountains, decided to stay.*

globe-encircling organization of multifaceted activities and international influence. It continually holds conferences involving a wide mix of academic, corporate, and political leaders in discussions about the most pressing issues of the day. It runs policy programs that draw the likes of former Presidents Jimmy Carter, George Bush, Bill Clinton, and former Prime Minister Margaret Thatcher, as well as Saudi Ambassador to Washington Prince Bandar, Queen Noor of Jordan, former secretary of state Henry Kissinger, the World Bank's James Wolfensohn, and Costa Rica's Nobel Laureate Oscar Arias Sanchez. The Institute also has drawn the interest of such European creative thinkers as Lionel Jospin, Johannes Rau, Roberto Toscano, Elio Catania, and Alexey Meshkovito. It hosts "executive seminars" to engage managers from highly diverse enterprises in philosophical discussions. It prints scores of publications filled with the work of its own researchers on how to better the world. The Aspen Institute sports a conspicuous political muscle, with offices in Washington, D.C., New York, and Chicago, as well as branches in France, Germany, Italy, and Japan. The office located on the Wye River on Maryland's Eastern Shore was the setting for a historic meeting between Israeli Prime Minister Benjamin Netanyahu and Palestinian leader Yasser Arafat. There are more than one hundred Aspen Institute Conferences each year, located around the world and dealing with such topics as the role of science in society, the changing relationships between men and women, re-thinking Europe, globalization, and monotheism among Jews, Christians,

ABOVE: *Reverberating with the haunting echo of the once silver-rich mining town—a boarded-up Victorian with broken stained glass—this artwork was exhibited at the Aspen Art Museum.*

and Moslems. Many of the Aspen Institute's board members spend a considerable part of the summer in Aspen in their dazzling second homes. They generously support the endless glamorous fundraising parties where some of America's most powerful and moneyed families —both Old and New—rub shoulders with crackerjack young entrepreneurs, movie stars, famous physicists and recording artists. They include the likes of Ann and William A. Nitze (a nephew of Paepke's), Ambassador and Mrs. Henry E. Catto, Iowa billionaires Kay and Matthew Buchsbaum, AOL-Time Warner's Gerald Levin, Texans Mercedes and Sid Bass, Leonard Lauder and his wife, Evelyn, and Michael Eisner and his wife, Jane.

Actual construction of today's permanent meeting facilities, townhouses, residential complex, lecture rooms, health center and the reception building (recently renovated thanks to a sizable donation from Prince Bandar) was begun in the early 1950s by Bayer in collaboration with his brother-in-law Fritz Benedict. Today, these Aspen Meadows buildings—all no-frills, utilitarian, and inexpensive —are also home to the Aspen Music Festival, the International Design Conference, and the Aspen Center of Physics. The Music Festival has lured the best musical talent in the world to perform beneath the Music Tent and staffs one of the top music schools in the country with such famous performing artists as Pinchas Zukerman, Joshua Bell, and Sarah Chang. Chang herself is one of the many young and gifted students, carefully sifted from notable music institutions around the world, who flock to Aspen each summer to play in three separate orchestras during the nine week programs. On summer days all of Aspen seems alive with the sound of rehearsing students' violins, flutes, pianos, and bassoons. Some mild evenings, students form impromptu quartets on the mall and play for tips in between performances at the Wheeler Opera or the Benedict Music Tent. Saarinen's original design for the tent was improved upon in 1964 by a Bayer-Benedict version, and again in 1997 by Aspen architect Harry Teague. This newest and perhaps most dazzling tent is constructed of state-of-the-art Teflon-coated fabric with a steel center disk; it's engineered to withstand Aspen's heavy snows and remains in place year-round.

Although the music, which is performed daily in the tent, is the heart and center of the Aspen summer, endless other artistic endeavors bring a non-stop wealth of culture to the tiny town. Aspen–Santa Fe Ballet is a nationally acclaimed ballet company, under the direction of Jean Philippe Malaty and Tom Mossbrucker, with its home in Aspen and a second residency in Santa Fe. Although it has an extensive national touring schedule of almost

OPPOSITE: *Uplifting to both mind and body, the lovely Aspen Meadows outside the Aspen Center for Physics are conducive to fine long walks, jogging, and biking.*

PAGE 106: *Jennifer Bartlett, Aspen 6 weeks, 1995.*

fifty performances in seventeen cities, it presents the Aspen Dance Festival every summer, which also features other world-renowned dance groups such as the Paul Taylor Dance Company. The Aspen Theater Company holds its own dramatic performances in yet another tent next to the Roaring Fork River. In a town that has always prided itself on freedom and independence, artistic self-expression is also alive and well at Jazz Aspen, born in 1991 in honor of the jazz tradition Aspen has embraced since the 1950s. The open-air jazz concerts held in Snowmass each August bring the world's most popular recording artists to Aspen. B. B. King, Diana Krall, Natalie Cole, Tony Bennett, and Ernie Watts are only a few of the visiting acts that attract growing audiences each year.

Aspen is also the site of numerous annual arts festivals, reflecting the creative predilections of many of its visitors. Each September a star or film-maker with a tie to the town of Aspen, such as Anjelica Huston or William H. Macy, is honored by the mayor with a series of film showings and dinner parties. In early April, Film Fest devotes a week to an international selection of short films by new and young filmmakers—but the most international of Aspen's festivals are the Food & Wine Classic, held in early June and the Design Conference held in late August. Hotels, restaurants, and condominiums overflow with innovators from every corner of the U.S.—especially New York, Chicago, and Los Angeles—as well as France, Italy, Germany, Russia, Canada, and Latin America. Held annually since 1951, the Design Conference is a week-long interdisciplinary gathering of architects, designers, photographers, art directors, and students that provoking thought and exploring the role of visual virtuosity in society. Likewise, the Food & Wine Classic has brought in wine connoisseurs, food critics and the world's top chefs each year since 1982. It features the likes of Jacques Pepin, Julia Child and Daniel Boulud, and seminars and lectures on international cuisines and wines. During this festival, eating is treated as one of the fine arts, and the center of Aspen becomes one open food mall of little tents featuring both tasty morsels and serious tastings. What started humbly as a city-slicker's "Aspen Idea" has grown into a thriving community that not only challenges its visitors' physical limitations but stimulates their creative and intellectual inclinations.

Artful Aspen

Crucial to Aspen's kinetic hum and hip reputation has been the town's longstanding and genuine interest in contemporary art. Over the years, Aspen has become a truly vibrant environment for both acclaimed and aspiring artists. They come in hordes, settling in for weeks or months: hot international art idols such as Eric Fischl, Jennifer Bartlett, Tim Hailand, David Salle, Dale Chihuly, David LaChapelle, and Ross Bleckner, make their annual pilgrimages, forsaking their metropolitan lofts for the lofty mountains. Inspiration is found in the refreshing scenery of rivers, lakes, rock formations, unusual flora, fauna, and, of course, some seriously discerning, art-buying residents. Aspen, with its urban sensibilities, restless disposition, novelty-loving tradition and, above all, knowledgeable and acquisition-minded citizenry, makes a perfect market for original visual statements. There are many people with deep pockets and large wall spaces on the lookout for the next hot thing.

At least three of Aspen's galleries have garnered international fame on par with the best of Manhattan's Chelsea or Madison Avenue and can strongly compete

New York artist Tim Hailand, famous for floating words above such landmarks as the Empire State Building, does a tongue-in-cheek interpretation of Aspen. In his Study for Smuggler Mountain, 2001, his inspiration is art dealer and man about Aspen, Harley Baldwin. Courtesy of the Baldwin Gallery.

LEFT TO RIGHT: *The Anderson Ranch Arts Center at Snowmass attracts both acclaimed and aspiring artists; Once an active mountain valley ranch, today the Anderson's ramshackle sheep sheds and cattle barns of the have become bucolic workshops for potters and photographers, and offer inspired introduction to the latest high-tech art materials; Both inside and out, the Aspen Institute is a fascinating repository of 20th-century art. Here,* Kaleidoscreen *by Herbert Bayer, the Bauhaus architect who left his mark on the Aspen Meadows topography via his large-scale colorful sculptures.*

with the fast-forward fare in such current art-buzz cities as Cologne or Milan, London or Basel. Their savvy owners display cutting-edge art and offer highly eclectic solo shows with elaborate receptions for the visiting artist. There is both a small-town intimacy and big-city frisson about these gatherings. Among the champagne-sipping art viewers might be resident movie star Kevin Costner, the latest Miss Universe or singer Diana Ross.

The Baldwin Gallery, under the aegis of Harley Baldwin and his Cambridge-educated lawyer partner Richard Edwards, serves up paintings, drawings, photography, and sculpture by the likes of James Rosenquist, David Salle, James Turrell, Alexis Rockman, Donald Baechler, Christo and Jeanne-Claude, Jennifer Bartlett, Enrique Martinez Celaya, Louise Nevelson, Robert Mapplethorpe, Elizabeth Murray, Donald Sultan, Mike and Doug Starn, Bryan Hunt, and Bruce Weber. Several of these highly creative artists have produced Aspen-themed visuals such as Tim Hailand's "Harleywood," which, featuring words floated over photos, is characteristic of his unique work. Harley Baldwin is one of the great Aspen success stories. A New York boy who made it big in the small Rocky Mountain town, he started out making crepes out of an old-fashioned popcorn wagon. He now owns the private Caribou Club, as well as the Brand Hotel and Caribou Jewels, and serves as landlord to a series of upscale European boutiques such as Dior, Frette, Gucci, Fendi, and Brioni.

On Mill Street, another high temple of contemporary art in all media, the David Floria Gallery exhibits both emerging and world-renowned artists such as Alice Neel, Ed Paschke, James Surls, Jody Guralnick, Caio Fonseca, Jose Bedia, Julio Galan, Brad Miller, and William Wegman. The list of internationals represented in the East Cooper Street Gallery belonging to Susan Duval includes Norwegian painter Bertil Valien, Dante Marioni, Dan Namingha, Dale Chihuly, Allison Stewart, and Scott Fraser.

The convergence of wave-making living artists and major art aficionados in Aspen started in 1966 when the Aspen Institute held a much-talked-about Pop Art exhibit that included works by Jasper Johns, Robert Rauschenberg, Roy Liechtenstein, James Rosenquist, and Andy Warhol. Spurred on by the success of the Pop Art exhibit and another Aspen exhibition of paintings by Willem de Kooning, the Aspen Center for Contemporary Art was formed. For the next three years, some of America's most audacious contemporary artists spent the summer months living it up in the ramshackle studios on the upper floors of the old Brand Building in the center of town. Among them were Rosenquist and Liechtenstein as well as Claes Oldenberg, Robert Indiana, Robert Morris, Les Levine, and DeWain Valentine. The presence of these urban bohemians, combined with the beginning of Aspen's hippie influx, added yet another spicy dimension to an already eclectic population.

The year 1966 also marked the birth of the Anderson Ranch Arts Center, which is today known around the world.

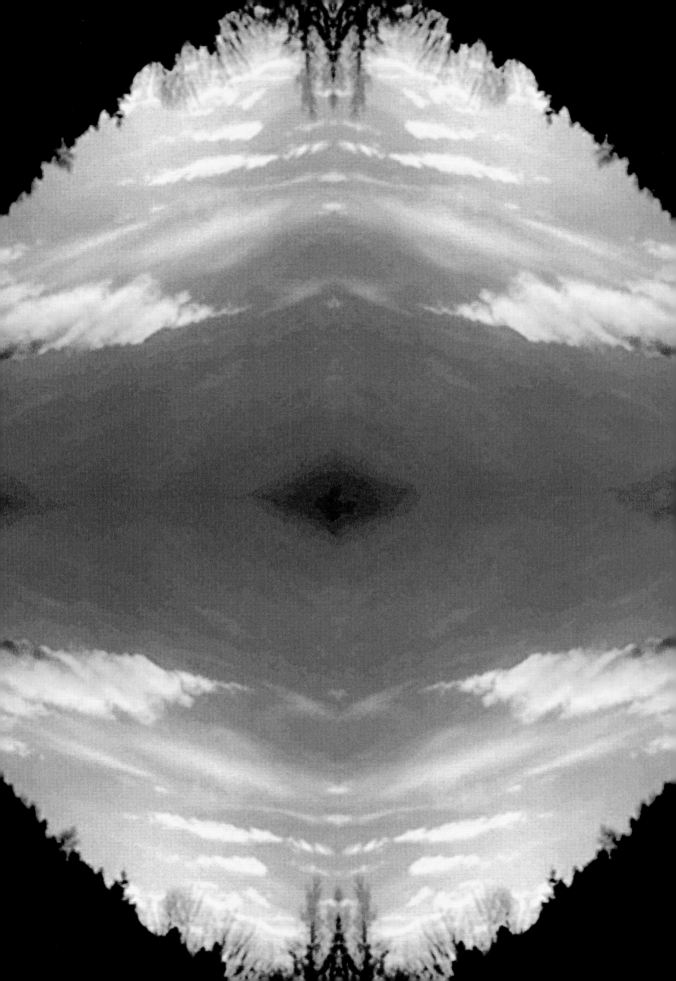

A sort of MacDowell Colony in Snowmass Village, part of Anderson Ranch's original agenda was to bring some summer amusement into the lives of ski-condominium and winter home owners in the then newly developed mountainside resort of Snowmass. The authentic Western-flavored, four-and-a-half acre Anderson Ranch is nowadays a bucolic meeting ground for painters, photographers, potters, printmakers, and woodworkers as well as art historians and critics. Legendary artists such as Jim Dine, Red Grooms, and Larry Rivers, as well as the well-known Japanese ceramist Takashi Nakazato, mix here with such celebrity students as Dennis Hopper, Dick Van Dyke, and B.B. King, who has stopped by after his performances at Jazz Aspen, which is held each August on the ranch. Gifted students come from as far as France and Greece, Iran and Nepal, as well as from inner cities in the United States. Between June and September about one thousand novices and professionals check in for two-week courses at the rustic scattering of cattle barns and sheep sheds, some dramatically modernized by architect Harry Teague with steel staircases and inventive modern lighting. They come to learn from experts, to learn from one another, or to explore new technologies in their respective fields. According to Anderson Ranch director Jim Baker, "We mainly offer workshops. Say, a short-term learning process of how to make a dovetail joint for an inexperienced beginner, or, for an established artist, the ranch might inspire ways to take the next step, discover a new level of creativity. We like to think of ourselves as a battery-charging place."

Annual Anderson Ranch fundraisers have become the most glamorous charity events in Aspen. They speak volumes about Aspen's dedication to contemporary art.

OPPOSITE: *Aspen social doyenne and art scene synergist Merrill Ford and retired Air Force general Robert Taylor in front of a Herbert Bayer tapestry they donated to the Denver Art Museum.*

PAGE 120: *Alexis Rockman,* Melva's Refrigerator, *2002. Courtesy of the Baldwin Gallery.*

PAGE 121: *Alexis Rockman,* Changing Places, *2002. Courtesy of the Baldwin Gallery.*

This dedication shows itself even more strongly in the support Aspen's powerful art collectors give to the year-round Aspen Art Museum. The marvelous high-ceilinged old brick building was Aspen's original hydroelectric power plant, serving until 1979 as a storage place for snowplows. It was then converted into the perfect gallery for the monumental sculptures and large-scale installations that characterized the 1970s. Under Dean Sobel, a former curator of contemporary art at the Milwaukee Art Museum and director of the Aspen Art Museum since 2000, this non-collecting cultural institution has set out to become a nationally and internationally recognized exhibition space in the idiom of such European Kunsthalles as the ones in Baden-Baden and Wiesbaden. Rather than competing with big-city museums for art acquisitions, the museum's objective is to mount highly original shows that will subsequently tour, thus bringing fame to the Aspen Art Museum. Already the museum's "Powder"—showcasing a vast variety of international artists' interpretations of the ephemeral substance—is considered one of the best shows in the country in recent years. So were a stylishly mounted show of Japanese baskets, "Bamboo Masterworks," and the one-man retrospectives of German artist Thomas Demand and the South African artist William Kentridge. Doubtless, all this good publicity has helped corral a fabulous roster for the museum's national council, which is a veritable A-list of philanthropists from every region of the United States.

The museum's behind-the-scenes who's who of generous givers includes high profile, part-time Aspen residents such as New Yorkers Ann Bass and Evelyn and Leonard Lauder. But the quiet big-moneyed Americans from Iowa and Illinois, Missouri and Ohio, Texas, California, and New York reveal even more about why Aspen has such educated tastes and high level of sophistication. There are Ann and Bill Nitze, who are also active with the National Gallery of Art in Washington D.C. and the Georgia O'Keefe Museum in Santa Fe. There are Susan and Larry Marx who have put together an amazing

OPPOSITE: The focus is on such artists as Andy Warhol, Jeff Koons, and Damien Hirst at the exhibition-only Aspen Art Museum, modeled on European Kunsthalles dedicated to global contemporary art.

personal art collection that includes a roomful of cat portraits by Andy Warhol as well as works by Jackson Pollock, Jean Dubuffet, Isamu Noguchi, Franz Kline, Eric Fischl, and Sigmar Polke. Jan and Ronald Greenberg of Louisiana serve as co-presidents of the Aspen Art Museum's National Council, a committee spearheaded by Chicago socialite Fran Dittmer, one of the most knowledgeable collectors of American art, Warhol, the minimalists, and today's top sculptors and painters. Also sitting on the council is Marina Forstmann Day, a Jungian analyst and sister of Wall Street entrepreneur Ted Forstmann; and Anderson Ranch board chairman Paul Schorr, head of a giant conglomerate of electrical construction in Lincoln, Nebraska. With his wife June, Schorr has amassed a far-famed art collection that includes works by Alexander Calder, Georgia O'Keefe, Adolph Gottlieb and Louise Bourgeois.

One of the most exciting aspects of life in Aspen is visiting the private realms of Aspenites who are involved with art to see how they live with their work. Artist Fay Peck's nude woodcuts climb to the raised ceiling of her busy living room, which also displays the many African masks and spears she's collected during a life of extensive travel. Inside Gitalong Ranch, the home of former Aspen Museum President Suzanne Farver, the whimsical, improbable and important all clamor for attention in the form of knitted cellophane (an Oliver Haring sculpture), a glittering sock (part of Liza Lou's Divorce Series called "Socks and Underwear"), and dramatic minimal installations by Dan Flavin and Donald Judd. In Harley Baldwin's splendid penthouse, atop a classic Victorian building in the center of town, two Indian portrait masterpieces of Chief Moanahonga and Chief Tshusick by Henry Inman celebrate the collector's eclectic flair in the company of ninth-century sculptures from Angkor Wat, a Richard Serra minimalist maquette, a row of Mapplethorpe photographs, and a Francesco Clemente triptych.

OPPOSITE: The Roaring Fork Valley with its rugged log cabins and inspiring wild scenery has always been supportive of creative young people and the bohemian lifestyle. Jane Jochem Hendricks, far right, with daughters Harmony, Hillary, and Heidi, who all know how to peel, plane and notch logs to build a home in the woods.

The Ranching Life

The ranch is the very essence of the Rocky Mountain West. It sums up the pioneering spirit. It embodies the rugged "can-do" mentality that drove American history across the vast unknown. "Home on the range" was—and is—a symbol of hope. It provided a hearth for the settlers in search of a better life. Standing alone on the endlessly unrolling frontier, it represented opportunity far from civilization, the luxury of freedom, the promise of independence, and a new lease on life. It is why people went west.

Nowadays in Aspen the ranching way of life is the realization of a similar dream for many former urbanites: the perfect atmospheric hideaway far from the hassle of the city. For second-home owners the ranch beckons as a healthy change of pace and an escape into wide-open spaces. Ranches are steeped in the spectacular changes of the seasons in the wild country, where coyotes cruise, ducks splash in the curve of a creek, and only the song of birds breaks the silence.

"Ever since I was a little boy and visited a dude ranch, I wanted to live out West," remembers Philadelphia commodities trader Wilton Jaffee. "At a very early age I knew I wanted to marry a rancher," recalls Pat Fender, who was brought up in

ABOVE: *A classic Western scene of horses in the snow-swept ranch country of Aspen where many of the Marlboro ads were photographed.*

OPPOSITE: *Fourth-generation Maroon Creek Valley rancher Rick Deane takes his family into town.*

PAGE 130: *Film producer Merv Adelson's authentic working horse barn with rusted-iron doors leading to each stall boasts wonderful Old West log-and-chink wainscoting. It was designed in the spirit of ranching Aspen by Zoe Compton.*

Connecticut, graduated from Vassar College, and is one of the "Women of Colorado's Roaring Fork Valley" lovingly portrayed by Meredith W. Ogilby in her book *A Life Well-Rooted*. She did end up marrying a Roaring Fork Valley rancher and has spent most of her adult life on a cattle ranch in Emma down the valley from Aspen. "It's hard to explain why ranching is such a compelling way of life to me and why it is so wrenching to know that it is vanishing. To see a new calf running in the sunshine on fields that are green because they were irrigated by your husband or son is a great pleasure. So is the sight of your daughter running out in a snowstorm to help her brother through the emergency chores. Ranching is a lifestyle rooted in nature."

Surrounded by mountain trails and corral fences, with horses running free in the snow, the ranch epitomizes the adventure of self-reliant characters who explored the Colorado wilderness and knew that winter was never far from the mountains. Originally, the tools used and the work to be done dictated a natural style for ranch living. In the early days, there were only the bare necessities: a roof overhead, a stove, and a bed. With the increase in the number of horses and cattle came the big functional tack room where saddles were tossed off, and chaps, lassos, and lariats hung on a wall full of hand-hewn wooden pegs. Stacked in the mudroom entrance were folded Navajo blankets and weather-beaten cowboy hats. Inside, old hickory rocking chairs placed before the big stone fireplace created cozy warmth on snowbound days. Traditional decor included lamps and furniture fashioned from antlers, snowshoes and sleighs, accented by posters, cigar-store wooden Indian figures, and Native American dolls. These days, whether it is a simple log cabin or a twelve-room field-stone family lodge, the Aspen-area ranch still embraces some of these classic Western features.

Zoning laws now prohibit people from keeping horses in the town of Aspen proper, so while the ranching style inspires boutiques and decorators in Aspen, today's authentic ranches are mostly tucked into the canyons of Old Snowmass. They spread along the south side of the valley's main highway in McLean Flats and in the still rough-and-ready river-coursed region of Woody Creek.

Definitely not Rodeo Drive, this is the real thing, including buckaroos and 55-gallon barrel races, held at the W/J Ranch, popular Aspen figure Wilton "Wink" Jaffee's old property on McLean Flats.

Ranching as a life-sustaining occupation has moved even farther down Aspen's Roaring Fork Valley to the towns of Emma, Basalt, and Carbondale, areas that have become major meccas for fly-fishermen as well.

As late as the 1960s, many of the houses on the north side of the Roaring Fork River were unadorned log cabins and farmhouses with splendid views of Capital Peak, Pyramid Peak, and Mt. Sopris. Back then ranchers often moved their cows and calves down Highway 82—the main thoroughfare between Glenwood Springs and Independence Pass—to graze on rented pasture for several weeks. Then the cattle would be trailed over the Carbondale bridge to rest overnight and, early the next morning, moved off to another pasture, hoping not to meet too many coal trucks on Highway 133.

ABOVE: *Determined to keep Woody Creek's ranching tradition alive, Ohio millionaire George Stranahan is one of Aspen's most-loved civic-minded activists.*

OPPOSITE: *The infamous Woody Creek Tavern, owned by George Stranahan and immortalized by gonzo journalist Hunter S. Thompson, where the likes of Jack Nicholson and Goldie Hawn hang out with the local cowboys and order the famous hamburger platter "with the works."*

PAGES 136-137: *Aspenite Lee Pardee in the breathtaking house he built out of all native materials in the unspoiled North Star Preserve.*

The ranching and farming era in Aspen—the period between the silver riches and the ski boom—is often referred to as "The Quiet Years." It was a difficult time, yet it rings with romance: the cowboys and herdsmen with their weathered faces and beaten-up cowboy hats and boots; the wide expanses of empty land and lonely roadways; the portraits of blue ribbon–winning bulls, prized cattle, and favorite horses. The poignant rhythm of branding the cows in spring and fall, roping the animals when they needed some doctoring, and the calving season, when as many as eight births took place in one night. The shoeing of the horses, the haying rituals, and the threshing machines. This image of life in the mountainous Old West was distilled brilliantly by Madison Avenue in the classic Marlboro cigarette ads, which were photographed mostly in the snow-heaped canyons of the Aspen region at places like the Christensen Ranch on Owl Creek, the Vagneur Ranch near Conundrum Creek, the Stranahan Ranch in Woody Creek, and the Marolt Ranch on the banks of Castle Creek. Aspen, unlike many other western silver boomtowns, never became a ghost town. The tough ranchers and farmers who loved the valley always saw it through its hard times.

One of the most colorful of these old ranching families is the Deane family of the T-Lazy-7 Ranch. Descendants of the first judge in Pitkin County, Joshua Deane, the family is famous for its spirited men and women who have been football stars and heroes of mountain rescue missions, dance-hall singers and stars of the silent screen. Rick Deane, the youngest of three brothers, now runs the ranch-breaking colts, taking guests on pack trips and fishing trips into the backcountry, and arranging breakfast horseback rides and dinner hayrides. In the evenings, he plays the guitar around the campfire. He is a real-life version of the cleft-jawed Marlboro man.

Today, much of Aspen is the domain of gentlemen ranchers—actors such as Kurt Russell, Kevin Costner, and Michael Douglas—who love to drop in and trade jokes with the real cowboys in the funky landmark Woody Creek Tavern. The amazing land they now own was developed by a previous generation of gentlemen ranchers such as former Navy Undersecretary and PanAm Vice President James Hopkins Smith, wealthy Chicagoans

In an atmospheric backcountry hideaway, faded old rodeo post-cards inside a weathered Western frame decorate a rustic log-cabin wall.

Autumn comes to the ranch.
Laurie McBride and her daughter,
Kate, a ski champion.

Henry Stein and Edgar Stern, and former Commerce Secretary and Houston oilman Robert Mosbacher. Much of the ranchland today is built around autumn hunts, polo games, equestrian events, and exclusive golf clubs such as The Maroon Creek Golf Club. Some, however, is still partially ranched by the likes of George Stranahan, who owns Woody Creek Tavern, or the Pfister family, who came to ski in the 1950s and settled on a vast track of land in Old Snowmass. Further down the valley is the sprawling Woody Creek, the horsy ranch country to which many of the Aspen Old Guard have retreated to live among their fabulous art collections in magnificent glass palaces with indoor rock gardens.

But, as Aspen-born Heidi Hendricks insists, "The West is still here. There is still land. So much land. Rejoice that you can still get lost. Would you believe that people still shoot at peoples' feet and tell them to 'Dance or get the hell out of here,' that people tie their hands to saddle horns thirteen miles from home 'cause they're so drunk and it's so dark and blizzarding so hard that if they fell off they'd be coyote meat. People still rope bears, walk ten miles for a measly Bloody Mary. Dive over bars and into liquor shelves headfirst. Trot thirty miles on horse with a broken leg. Climb a 12,000 foot mountain to slide down on a trash bag cause there is no TV to watch, no computers to play on. There are still places where you are so alone that you go outside and scream, and nine times out of ten a dozen coyotes will answer you, reassuring you that you're not alone. Didn't want you people up North, down South, back East to worry: there is a place that is the West and it's still pretty Western."

PAGE 142: *At the center of ranch life is the oversized hearth crafted out of indigenous rock. This one faces an antler chandelier and is surrounded by Navajo rugs.*

PAGE 143: *God Bless America! A homey picket-fence bed, a handmade country quilt, and stars and stripes above.*

OPPOSITE: *Remote and romantic: The Rocky Mountain ranch with its unique Western-style fence trailing off into the horizon is as much a state of mind as a real place.*

Always a Pioneer of Styles

Nowhere has the fantasy of the American Dream flourished as it has in Aspen. Its varied meaning is vividly played out in how Aspen lives today. The inventive Rocky Mountain homes scattered up and down the meadows, mesas, and canyons along the Roaring Fork Valley are truly awesome. Meanwhile, the lifestyles of the people who live in them often make headlines far beyond Aspen.

Aspen is home to both craftsmen opting to be loners in cow-camp cabins deep in the woods and overnight billionaires hoping to validate themselves by building on a lavish scale. As much as it tries to deny it, Aspen is a capital of capitalism, with a proud legacy of those who made it big. Powerful men and women come here to mingle and play games of one-upmanship. Throwing big parties in big houses for local charities attracts the attention of those who count. This group's motto tends to be "bigger is better."

The dream house in Aspen can take spectacular shapes. There's the soaring white abode that was built for Cher—a real dazzler of a house, in some ways resembling a great phantasmagoric mushroom. It was the first home anywhere to feature a "safe room." There was the otherworldly steel-and-glass house on

ABOVE: *Charismatic and handsome Aspen ski champion Spyder Sabich had just launched his line of snappy skiwear when he was murdered in the shower by his lover, French actress Claudine Longet.*

OPPOSITE: *Aspen's original inhabitants, the Jute Indians, with their insouciant swagger and love of horsemanship, demonstrate how from the start Aspen had plenty of style.*

Red Mountain, with its lights ever twinkling, looking as if it were about to take off on some outer galactic mission. Until it burned down, it belonged to Frank Butler, the outrageously eccentric heir to Butler Aviation who used to make grand entrances at parties wearing a white Travolta suit, Dracula cape and mink Cossack hat. Another Aspen original is the home of former Playboy playmate Barbi Benton. This giant mountain palace is made of copper that was supposed to oxidize with age and turn greenish but instead took on the reddish sheen of a freshly minted U.S. penny. Inside Barbi Benton's modern fairytale house another series of fantasies come to life, such as the funky entertainment room with a giant, vividly colored fish tank. There's also Cassandra Lohr's Western fantasy of a "tamed teepee"; pitched by the side of a mountain lake it holds a bedroom, office, and entertainment center within the twenty-eight-foot diameter of a conical canvas enclosure. It's both rugged and refined, with electricity, hardwood floors, and an authentic American Indian fire pit in the center. The fire pit, in turn, is surrounded by a Victorian fringed chaise of steer horns and cowhide, a big Wyoming burl-fir bed dressed with Ralph Lauren bedding, and Sioux bows and arrows, as well as leather crafts by North African Tuareg tribes. Former New Yorker Travis Fulton, handsome bachelor and descendent of steamboat inventor Robert Fulton, lives in a backwoods log cabin where he crafts minimalist bronze sculptures and has little more than an old-fashioned wood-burning iron stove to keep his hands from freezing. One of Aspen's most beloved couples, Kenny and

LEFT TO RIGHT: *The quintessence of Aspen aprés-ski: sun, snow, beautiful girls, handsome men, libation and flirtation in an incomparable Western setting; Although they were known as "the quiet years" when Aspen went from silver boom to bust, Aspenites never stopped having fun. Here, a Sunday outing on wooden skis circa 1900; Successfully demonstrating how the lure of the wilderness and the trappings of civilization can blissfully co-exist has always been at the crux of Aspen's savoir-vivre.*

Betty Moore, did something similar thirty years ago. They were part of a group of clean-cut, all-American college grads from well-off East Coast families who came to Aspen as ski bums when there was only one chair lift to whisk people uphill for a day's skiing. Kenny and Betty decided to stay and opened the old Tippler Inn as a bed-and-breakfast at the base of Aspen Mountain. In time they built a rambling modern ranch for themselves using local wood and stone from the nearby creek. Inside this strikingly original wood-beamed labyrinth, they managed to encapsulate many fantasies. Not the least of these is the sky-lit sunken living room modeled after a Mediterranean village square where bougainvillea, jasmine, and pots of lavender bloom all winter long around the huge fieldstone fireplace.

What happens before and after these houses are attained is both lore and legend. For example, Enron chief Kenneth Lay owned four big houses in Aspen and sold them all within a month, before the end of the year in which Enron's collapse became a scandal. A few years after the Berlin Wall fell, a scam artist from Prague—oozing with charm, crazy with cash, and known for giving lavish soirées—swindled some of Aspen's savviest financiers out of $22 million.

When everyone from the great metropolises is in town for Christmas or the Music Festival, parties abound. Spanish grandees, Arab princes, Venezuelan and Brazilian tycoons, all of whom attend the most glamorous black-tie parties in the palatial houses of Red Mountain and Starwood, represent a real international

THIS PAGE: *Pitching a Native American–style teepee in the wide open spaces is one way of living close to nature in Aspen.*

OPPOSITE: *The Western fantasy of a teepee need not mean forsaking the creature comforts of a fringed Victorian chaise longue and a bed dressed by Ralph Lauren.*

LEFT TO RIGHT: *One of the most admired women in Aspen, Betty Pfister used her candy-colored helicopter in the '70s for both mountain rescues and swooping up guests for extravagant picnics in hidden mountain valleys; Gamboling in the snow with her mastiff, Lita Warner Heller is the grande dame of Aspen and its many charity events. She is Hollywood royalty, daughter of one of the original Warner Brothers; It was her love of big dogs and horses that inspired her to settle in Aspen in the early '70s.*

who's who. Marshall Field heir and Hollywood producer Ted Field once employed twelve guards for a star-studded Aspen Foundation benefit given in his extravagant, ten-room house filled with Maltese chandeliers and Burmese antiques. Bill Joy, the founder of Sun Micro-systems, and Les Wexner of The Limited entertain in their enormous houses but ban press coverage. The newest no-holds-barred party-throwers are Betsy and James Fifield—Betsy was an advertising executive in New York when she met Jim Fifield, former president of E.M.I. records in England—whose benefit for New Medicine in their breathtaking candlelit solarium was one of the most enchanting evenings Aspen society has seen. Created by Brazilian architect Horatio Bavazzani, the glass-enclosed box in the center of the huge house is a brilliant green tangle of jungle trees and tropical flowers. On the night of the benefit, a magical snowscape lay outside the glass: a full moon illuminating heaps of white stuff, the black silhouette of the mountains in the distance. The couple's life revolves around a London flat, a Tribeca loft and the Aspen house—of which the most amusing feature is the jewel-like dining room done by British decorator André Dubreuil, who is famous for his spine chair in the Victoria and Albert Museum in London.

Trying to get into Mary Eshbaugh Hayes' "Around Aspen" social column in the *Aspen Times* is the secret hope of every Aspen party-giver and party-goer. An Aspen original if ever there was one, with her huge glasses framing elfin eyes that miss nothing, the Liz Smith of Aspen knows everything that

goes on. But she is never nasty. "Oh, you could never get away with that in a small town like this," she says.

Unquestionably, the grand dame of Aspen Society is Lita Warner Heller. Born into one of the first families of cinema, she is the leading lady of the fund-raising circuit, especially for ballet, music, and the performing arts. She is the daughter of Sam Warner, one of the founders of Warner Brothers, and Lina Basquette, a Ziegfield Follies girl turned silent film star. Lita's father was the first to develop sound for film but died tragically the day before the premiere of his crowning achievement, *The Jazz Singer*. After an extended custody battle with Lita's beautiful mother, Harry Warner, the feared and admired head of Warner Brothers, became Lita's legal guardian. When Warner bought Calabases, a large, 100-horse ranch located north of Los Angeles, for filming Westerns, he introduced Lita to riding. In 1973, a serendipitous trip to Aspen with her second husband, banker and developer Mort Heller, made Lita realize that a Woody Creek ranch would make a good home for someone with horses and big dogs (seven bull mastiffs and three English mastiffs). Despite her life of extraordinary privilege, Lita has always had a keen sense of social responsibility. She became president of Ballet Aspen even while riding with the Roaring Fork Hounds club and raising five children. She then, along with French-born New Yorker Christine Aubel Gerschel, founded Les Dames d'Aspen, a group of well-connected women who raised two million dollars for scholarships and various art organizations in the Roaring Fork Valley.

Next in line to be the reigning catalyst of Aspen's social scene are a number of formidable women who throw splendid parties in splendid houses and have lent enormous brainpower and style to Aspen's many causes. Tall, blonde art collector Frannie Dittmer, a Texan who came to Aspen via a Washington, D.C. career and a Lake Forest fortune, has been particularly active in Aspen's art circles. Paepke relation and Washington socialite Ann Nitze's interests include the Aspen Institute and Music Festival. Susan Marx hails from Santa Monica and is a former head of the national board of the Aspen Museum, whose cause is the struggle of immigrant workers in down-valley Aspen. From Knoxville comes is Sandy Bishop whose big at-home fundraisers are legendary. Diane Anderson of Mexico City sits on the board of at least five important organizations and hosted several memorable benefits at the Mountain Club on top of Aspen Mountain.

It is not surprising, then, that Aspen is one of a handful of U.S. communities consistently ahead of the crest. If it happens big all over, it often happens in Aspen first. Aspen was Colorado's hottest mining town in the days when the mountains of this country were spawning millionaires. It was the first international high-alpine ski resort in America. It may even have been the pioneer of snowboards, despite years of banning them from the slopes; a *Life* magazine feature from March 1965 reports that kids from California beaches rocked the slopes with wild skiing on surfboards. Aspen was also the first mountain town to have a large New Age community and the first to have helicopter picnics in hidden valleys, a notion pioneered by ranchers Art and Betty Pfister. Aspen is still the only town to have had three "hippie" mayors in a row, two of whom have posed naked for magazine centerfolds.

While the characters in Aspen have changed, one thing has remained the same: The people who make up Aspen are consistently amusing, never dull. Over the years, sprinklings of scandals have spiced up Aspen's image as a place of unbridled passion and relatively light punishment. Most notorious of these was the 1972 murder of popular ski champion Spyder Sabich. He was gunned down in the shower after he tried to break off an affair with French singer Claudine Longet, who at the time was married to American pop recording star and Kennedy-family friend

Andy Williams. Claudine was tried for the "crime of passion" and went to prison for one month, after which she came back to Aspen and married her defense lawyer (breaking up his marriage). Another case of jealous rage involved two world-famous Asian beauties at a glittering New Year's Eve party at a nightclub. Feeling upstaged by Philippine heiress Minnie Osmena, Dewi Sukarno, the former wife of the president of Indonesia, suddenly smashed the champagne flute she was sipping from and slashed Minnie's pretty face with the broken glass. Dewi was tried and incarcerated in Aspen for two months; every afternoon, however, she was permitted to take her water-color easel to scenic Hallam Lake. At the end of her imprisonment, one of Aspen's galleries gave her a vernissage and nearly all her paintings sold. Perhaps the most famous American divorce of the last quarter century broke from Aspen into tabloid headlines. Donald Trump was left to do some fancy footwork when Ivana Trump and Marla Maples came face to face at high noon on the sundeck at the top of Aspen Mountain.

Donald Trump, of course, was pretty high profile in Aspen during much of the glitzy eighties. He was part of the battle that best exemplified the struggle for the soul of Aspen: the fight over a five-star hotel to be built at the foot of Aspen Mountain. Never was the town's reputation for "spirited public debate" more in evidence. The subject dominated public meetings and barrooms for nearly a decade. Two of the original would-be developers went bankrupt before the colorful Mohamed Hadid, along with the Ritz-Carlton, swept the property out from under Trump's feet. The resplendent red-brick, 600-room structure that finally did go up in 1995 combines a touch of Aspen's Victorian architecture with something resembling a Bavarian baronial castle. The Ritz abruptly became the St. Regis in 1997 when, while the hotel was filled with guests, the entire Ritz-Carlton group of executives packed up and disappeared. Despite the commotion, today people are glad to have the luxury hotel. In fact, Aspen has a real need for ballrooms and sparkling settings now that big-city charities have landed in the little mountain village. For the many non-profit organizations forming the base of the town's cultural heritage, the number of fund-raisers has increased.

Ultimately, Aspen is more than a town and more than a resort playground; it is also an experiment in living. In recent years it has collected garlands of mocking sobriquets and idealizing hyperboles: from "Hollywood in the Rockies" to the "last wild cry for freedom"; from "an exercise in hedonism" to "the ultimate escape"; from "Disneyland for adults" to "the most tolerant and

PAGE 156: *Mogul chic: "The bigger the better" is the motto of Aspen architects and their many CEO clients who build their houses to impress.*

OPPOSITE: *The height of luxury: An Aspen slope-side mansion has palatial features in its grand entrance hall, such as a resplendent Maltese chandelier, a Burmesse table, and an ornate mezzanine.*

honest town in America." The growth that took place in Aspen between 1960 and the end of the twentieth century was nothing short of phenomenal. The population of the city itself increased by more than 500 percent. The population of Pitkin County, an oddly shaped territory encompassing 960 square miles between Independence Pass and the rural townships of Basalt and Carbondale, has grown even more dramatically. As one weary community activist put it, "A valley less loved would have been ruined."

Conflicts sometimes come into particularly sharp focus because of the size of the place. All the beauty and ugliness that gets lost in a big city tends to be accentuated in tiny Aspen. Left up to the volatile demands of an invading affluent society, Aspen's future seems always in precarious balance. Writes Sally Barlow-Perez in *A History of Aspen*: "Short of putting a gate across Highway 82 that said 'No More New Residents Permitted' (the idea was discussed with some seriousness), there was no way to stop the flow. The immediate attraction was evident: an incredibly beautiful valley in the heart of some of the earth's finest ski country. But newcomers were drawn for far more complicated reasons. Urbanites and suburbanites all over the country evinced longing for 'community,' for the sense of belonging that a small town might deliver."

Aspen means many things to many people: the romance of danger, the delights of dalliance, the culture maven's smorgasbord, the outdoorsman's paradise. It's the winter crossroads of international nomads and a summer throb of concerts, conferences, and classes. It's the ultimate in Rocky Mountain High—and sometimes Low. It's a place that has been famous for easy sex and drugs. A place to which the newly divorced flock to reassemble egos, reenact adolescent fantasies, and rebuild lives—and then a place from which they run, in search of a simpler frontier-town somewhere in Idaho or New Mexico. Aspen may be studied Stetson and deliberate denim, but it is also wholesome all-American families piling in and out of four-wheel drives, trekking to Independence Pass, cross-country skiing through the woods, and riding the chairlifts of Snowmass. It is cowboys hanging around saloons with scruffy musicians who are waiting to be discovered.

The clear mountain air, the untamed and ungroomed slopes, the chance to test one's personal limits, and the singular character of the town continue to lure the full range of American achievers to Aspen.

OPPOSITE: *Originally designed for pop diva Cher, this extraordinary living room is dominated by a giant stylized adobe chimney and commands a 360-degree panoramic view of the dazzling Rocky Mountains.*

Bibliography

Allen, James Sloan. *The Romance of Commerce and Culture: Capitalism, Modernism, and the Chicago-Aspen Crusade for Cultural Reform.* Chicago: The University of Chicago Press. 1983.

Andersen, Paul and Ohlrich, Warren H. *Aspen: Portrait of a Rocky Mountain Town.* Aspen: WHO Press. 1992.

Andersen, Paul. *East of Aspen: A Field Guide to Independence Pass and the Upper Roaring Fork Valley.* ERG Press. 2001.

Andersen, Paul and Ohlrich, Warren H. *Aspen in Color: Seasons of a Mountain Town.* Aspen: WHO Press. 1990.

Barlow-Perez, Sally and Ohlrich, Warren H. *A History of Aspen.* Aspen: WHO Press. 2002.

Bowen, Ezra. *The Book of American Skiing.* J.B. Lippincott Company. 1963.

Clifford, Peggy and Smith, John M., *Aspen/Dreams & Dilemmas.* Chicago: The Swallow Press, Inc. 1970.

Clifford, Peggy. *To Aspen and Back: An American Journey.* New York: St. Martin's Press. 1980.

Daily, Kathleen Krieger and Guenin, Gaylord T. and Borneman, Diane. *Aspen: The Quiet Years.* Red Ink Inc. 1994.

Drinkard, G. Lawson, III. *Retreats: Handmade Hideaways to Refresh the Spirit.* Layton, Utah: Gibbs-Smith. 1997.

Farver, Suzanne and Feldman, Suzanne and Hobbs, Robert. *20 Years/20 Artists.* Aspen: Aspen Art Museum. 2000.

Flood, Elizabeth Clair. *Rocky Mountain Home: Spirited Western Hideaways.* Layton, Utah: Gibbs-Smith. 1996.

Hayes, Mary Eshbaugh. *Aspen Potpourri: The People, Places and Food of Aspen.* Aspen: Aspen Potpourri. 1996.

Hayes, Mary Eshbaugh and Cassatt, Chris. *The Story of Aspen.* Aspen: Aspen Three Publishing. 1997.

Livingston, Kathryn. *Victorian Interiors.* Glouchester, Massachusetts: Rockport Publishers Inc. 1999.

Lum, Su and Lewis, Barbara A. *Fisher the Fixer.* Aspen: The Aspen Times. 1973.

Ogilby, Meredith W. *A Life Well Rooted: Women of Colorado's Roaring Fork Valley.* Hell-Roaring Publishing. 2002.

Ohlrich, Warren H. *Aspen: In Celebration of the Aspen Idea.* Aspen: WHO Press. 1999.

Ohlrich, Warren H. *Aspen Snowmass Trails: Hiking Trail Guide.* Aspen: WHO Press. 1997.

O'Rear, John and Frankie. *The Aspen Story.* New York: A.S. Barnes and Co., Inc. 1966.

Pfeifer, Friedl and Lund, Morten. *Nice Goin': My Life on Skis.* Missoula, Montana: Pictorial Histories Publishing Company, Inc. 1993.

Acknowledgments

I would like to express my deepest thanks to Ellen Nidy of Assouline Publishing, the editor of this book, whose fine-honed editorial instincts and passion for the story-telling photograph steered this project through its various visual and verbal challenges. Her level-headedness, indefatigable enthusiasm and always-gracious ways were never less than inspiring. I'm also indebted to Ausbert d'Arce, who saw my last book and introduced me to Martine and Prosper Assouline. My special thanks to Martine, whose sense of style and immediate grasp of Aspen's quirky elegance led to the opportunity to do this book. And to Prosper, whose superb eye for the witty image and clever ideas on juxtaposing bygone flair against the hipness of contemporary culture—along with the design savvy of Mathilde Dupuy d'Angeac—set the tone for this book. My appreciation also goes to assistant editor Caitlin Leffel, whose copyediting sharpened the text.

At the core of this volume lies the talent of many photographers, artists, architects, interior designers, and above all, the outpouring of goodwill from stellar Aspenites who let me invade their private photo albums, and allowed me to whisk some cherished family mementos off their walls for use in this book. *In the Spirit of Aspen* would not have been possible without the scrapbooks and insights of Ken and Betty Moore, Jackie Wogan, Miggs and Dick Durrance, Betty Pfister, Klaus Obermeyer, Lita Warner Heller, Ashley Anderson, Frannie Dittmer, Harry Teague, Linda Niven, Fay Peck, Susan and Larry Marx, Frederick Selby, David Koch, Betty Landreth, Ann Ferrell, jewelry designer Karen Mitchell, custom-shirt maker Tadine, hot-shot downhillers Patrick Burke and Michael Tiedemann, Andy Modell of the Aspen Catalog, Susan Duval and her husband Robert McGregor, extreme skiing's ambassador to the world Chris Davenport, who bumped into Robin Williams, Danny DeVito, and Whoopi Goldberg during our interview at the Hotel Jerome; Ute Indian Nation activist Connie Marlow, Phyllis and Grafton Smith, Nora Feller and her food-connoisseur husband, Francois Couturier, Nora Berko Mallory, Merrill Ford, Michael Lipkin, Kathryn Fleck, Hildegard Jones, Becky Green, Julia Hansen, Jack Crawford, Terry Butler, Heidi Hendrick, Meredith Ogilby, Olympic-medal snowboarder Chris Klug and his proud Aspen father, Warren Klug; the Aspen Music Festival's president Don Roth, the Aspen Art Museum's head Dean Sobel; Richard McLennan and Jenn Stanley of the St. Regis Aspen Hotel, Eric Calderon, Jane Stapleton, and John Egelhoff of the Little Nell Hotel; Dick Butero, Jennifer Brasington, and Steven Holt of the Hotel Jerome; Lukey Seymour, Diane Williams, and Susan Crown for a most helpful mountaintop lunch next to the baronial fireplace at the Aspen Mountain Club. Warmest appreciation to my long-time New York friends Mary and George Kirkham, who introduced me to the whole new, happening scene down-valley in Carbondale and Basalt; and to my much respected former-Aspenite friends Mary and General William Martin, who were instrumental in the launching of Snowmass and the Anderson Ranch Arts Center. They have been there for me with astute advice and unceasing help from the beginning of this project.

My greatest gratitude goes to man-about-Aspen Harley Baldwin and his Baldwin Gallery. Harley, whom I met at Jennifer Bartlett's Greenwich Village loft, took me by the hand in Aspen, got me invited to the best parties in town, and helped open all the most glamorous doors, to the advantage of these pages.

No one knows more about Aspen than Mary Eshbaugh Hayes of the *Aspen Times* or Janet O'Grady, editor in chief of *Aspen Magazine*. I shall be indebted to them both forever for their generous sharing of precious background material, pertinent, up-to-date information, and their journalistic front-row-center personal observations.

To the Aspen Ski Company, especially communications coordinator Melissa Rhines, as well as freestyle skiers Billy O'Donnell and Alex Potter. Many thanks for the energy, kindness, and chance to glimpse the latest doings on the mountain and après-ski. Thanks to everyone at The Aspen Historical Society, where I spent many long hours, wearing white protective gloves, looking through ancient photographs as well as more recent documents. To Christine Nolen of the Aspen Chamber of Commerce: thank you so much for timelines, statistics, and key directional ideas.

Finally, I would like to thank my sister-in-law, Sissy Wheeler of Lake Forest. She was a friend of the legendary Mrs. Elizabeth Paepke of Chicago and volunteered to make several invaluable Aspen introductions for me. Fond appreciation goes to my brother Stephen Zahony, a Colorado-based exploration geologist, who helped me with topography maps and tales of silver mining days and ghost towns on Colorado's Western Slopes. To my good friend John Fry, revered former editor of *Ski* and *Snow Country* magazines, thanks for being a walking encyclopedia of the history of skiing. Best of all, hugs and kisses to my children, Bret and Valerie, both skiers from the time they were three-year-olds. Their love of fresh powder snow, big blue skies, rock, and ice pushed me to become a better outdoors person, which, in turn, led to some of the best times of my life.

Photo credits

Cover: courtesy Frederick Selby private archives; back cover: Grafton Marshall Smith; pp.6-7: David O. Marlow; p.9: Nora Feller; pp.10-11: Mary Eshbaugh Hayes; p.12: courtesy Fay Peck private archives; p.14: Nora Feller; p.15: Grafton Marshall Smith; p.16: courtesy Aspen Historical Society; p.17: courtesy Aspen Historical Society; p.18: Frederick Selby; p. l9: courtesy Art and Betty Pfister private archives; p.20: Mary Eshbaugh Hayes; p.21: Mary Eshbaugh Hayes; p.22: David O. Marlowe; p.23: courtesy Aspen Historical Society; pp.24-25 top left: courtesy Aspen Historical Society; top center: courtesy Jackie Wogan private archives; top right: Mary Eshbaugh Hayes; p.26: Bettina Mueller; p.27: David O. Marlow; p.28: Chris Cassatt; pp.30-31: All rights reserved; p.32: Grafton Marshall Smith; p.33: courtesy Sport Obermeyer, Ltd. USA; pp.34-35: top left: Mary Eshbaugh Hayes; top center: David O. Marlow; top right: Mary Eshbaugh Hayes; pp.36-40: photos courtesy Aspen Historical Society; p.42: courtesy Mary and George Kirkham; p.43: Grafton Marshall Smith; p.44: Frank Martin; p.45: Grafton Marshall Smith; pp.46-47: David O. Marlow; p.49: Nora Feller; p.50: courtesy Mary Kirkham; pp.52-53, clockwise: Mary Eshbaugh Hayes, photo Gretl Uhl; Barclay Tuck hiking up Aspen Highlands Ridge, courtesy Tadine private archives; David Stickelberg Kansas City and Frannie Dittmer Lake Forest, photo courtesy Fay Peck private archives; Beth Ann Christensen and Tadine: Robert McGregor and Susan Duval with their children: Nora Feller; Stein Eriksen: Mary Eshbaugh Hayes; Bari Rosen and friends at Aspen Highlands, Tadine in ski goggles: both photos courtesy Tadine private archives; p.54: Mary Eshbaugh Hayes; p.55: Kevin Lein; pp.56-57: courtesy Jackie Wogan private archives; pp.58-59: courtesy Harley Baldwin and the Caribou Club; pp.60-61: top left: courtesy Aspen Historical Society; top center and top right: Mary Eshbaugh Hayes; p.62: Mary Eshbaugh Hayes; pp.62-63: courtesy the Hotel Jerome; p.64: Jeffrey Aaronson/Network Aspen, all rights reserved; p.65: Mary Eshbaugh Hayes; p.66: caricature courtesy the Caribou Club; p.67: Nora Feller; p.68: courtesy St. Regis Aspen Hotel; p.70: courtesy Frederick Selby private archives; p.71: courtesy Frederick Selby private archives; p.72: courtesy the Aspen Historical Society; pp.72-73: Mary Eshbaugh Hayes; p.74: Nora Feller; pp.76-77 clockwise from left to right: Aspen al fresco eating at the Main Street Bakery: Nora Feller; Catherine Zeta-Jones, Michael Douglas, Denise Rich, Marty Richards and friend at Aspen New Year's Eve party: Nora Feller, all rights reserved; Ivana Trump and pals: Frederick Selby; Aspen's trademark street lamps at central mall: Nora Feller; Goldie Hawn flexing muscles: Frederick Selby; Minnie Osmana and friends making a toast: Frederick Selby; Harley Baldwin at the entry to the Caribou Club, courtesy the Caribou Club; hotel heiress Nicky Hilton with Harley Baldwin: Nora Feller; Sean Connery with David Koch: courtesy Frederick Selby private archives; Arne Naess, Diana Ross, and David Koch: Frederick Selby; Charles Dale: Nora Feller, all rights reserved; p.78: Grafton Marshall Smith; p.79: Grafton Marshall Smith; pp.80-81: Grafton Marshall Smith; p.82; David O. Marlow; p.83: Jeffrey Aaronson/Network Aspen, all rights reserved; p.84: John Russell/Network Aspen; pp.86-87: clockwise from top left: rafters, Grafton Marshall Smith; bride Stephanie Woods with her flower girls: courtesy Sandra Woods private archives; El Jabal pheasant shoot with Art and Betty Pfister: Grafton Marshall Smith; trout fishing near bridge: Cindy Crawford at Silver Lining Ranch benefit for children with leukemia: Nora Feller; Ann Ferrell delighted with her catch: courtesy Ann Ferrell private archives; Aspen veteran ski racers, circa l956: Friedl Pfeiffer, Fred Iselin, Dick Durrance, and Pete Seibert: courtesy Aspen Historical Society; balloons over Snowmass: Frederick Selby; three-year-old Madison Shea and teenagers in jeep, both photos courtesy Fay Peck private archives; world-famous fly-fisherman, guide and best-selling author, Chuck Fothergill: Grafton Marshall Smith; p.88: All rights reserved, courtesy the Aspen Art Museum; p.89: *The Scene Outside the Aspen Music Tent*, hand-colored etching by Adair Peck, 1988, courtesy Fay Peck; pp.90-91: Ferenc Berko, courtesy Aspen Institute; p.92: Nora Feller; p.93: © Margaret Durrance; p.94: Chris Cassatt photo; p.95: Chris Cassatt photo; p.96: Goethe Bicentennial Souvenir Program cover, 1949, courtesy the Aspen Institute; p.97: Ferenc Berko, courtesy the Aspen Institute; p.98: All rights reserved, from the Container Corporation America Poster Collection, courtesy the Smithsonian Institute; p.99: Burnham Arndt, photographer, courtesy International Design Conference in Aspen; pp.100-101: top left: Ferenc Berko; top center: Nora Feller, courtesy the Aspen Institute; top right: Ferenc Berko, all rights reserved; pp.102-103: Ferenc Berko, courtesy Aspen Art Museum; p.105: All rights reserved, courtesy the Aspen Institute; pp.106-107: Jennifer Bartlett, *Independence Pass*, 1996, courtesy the

Baldwin Gallery; pp.108-109, clockwise from top left: Anjelica Huston and Hollywood agent Martha Luttrell: Mary Eshbaugh Hayes; World Bank president James Wolfensohn: Nora Feller, courtesy the Aspen Institute; violinist Pinchus Zuckerman: Nora Feller; conductor Claudio Scimone heading to the Aspen Music Festival tent on bicycle: Nora Feller; actors Felicy Huffman and her husband, William H. Macy, at the Aspen Film Fest: Nora Feller; jogger: Mary Eshbaugh Hayes; violin prodigy Sarah Chang at age eight, performing in the Aspen Music Festival tent: Nora Feller; Terry Butler and former president Jimmy Carter at an Aspen Institute benefit: Mary Eshbaugh Hayes; center photograph: left to right: Aspen Institute board member Ann Hudson, Walt Disney chairman Michael Eisner, and Marlene Malek: Nora Feller; pp.110-111: David O. Marlow; pp.112-113: courtesy Baldwin Gallery; pp.114-115 top left and center: courtesy the Anderson Ranch Arts Center; far right: Mary Eshbaugh Hayes; p.116: courtesy the Baldwin Gallery; p.117: courtesy the Baldwin Gallery; pp.118-119: photograph courtesy Merrill Ford personal archives; p.120: courtesy the Baldwin Gallery, Aspen; p.121: courtesy the Baldwin Gallery; pp.122-123: Warhol, Koons, Hirst: Selections from the Vicky and Kent Logan Collection, courtesy the Aspen Art Museum; pp.124-125: Meredith Ogilby, all rights reserved; pp.126-127 clockwise from top left: painting by Jennifer Bartlett, courtesy Baldwin Gallery; potter Takashi Nakazato, courtesy the Anderson Ranch Arts Center; The Ice Palace, a commune for struggling young artists and craftsmen in a rickety old Victorian house: Chris Cassatt. Stairway: Gibson Architects, David O. Marlowe; Aspen grande dame Mrs. Elizabeth Paepke with artist Fay Peck, at the exhibit of her work in the Hotel Jerome in 1976: courtesy Fay Peck private archives; the nearly lost art ice sculpture at Snowmass Mountain, contest sponsored by the Anderson Ranch Arts Center, courtesy Anderson Ranch Arts Center; Kevin Costner with Harley Baldwin: Nora Feller , courtesy the Baldwin Gallery; p.128. Grafton Marshall Smith; p.129: Grafton Marshall Smith; pp.130-131: David O. Marlow; p.132: Grafton Marshall Smith; p.133: Grafton Marshall Smith; p.134: Nora Feller; pp.134-135: Nora Feller; 136-137: Grafton Marshall Smith; pp.138-139: Peter Woloszynski; pp.140-141: Meredith Ogilby, all rights reserved; p.142: Peter Woloszynski; p.143: Peter Woloszynski; p. 45: David O. Marlow; pp.146-147, clockwise from top left: the tack room at Adelson ranch designed by Zoe Compton: David O. Marlow; Aspen polo player at McLain Flats polo field: Grafton Marshall Smith; Aspen ranch kitchen: David O. Marlow; Rocky Mountain-style kitchen barstool from Spence Collections, Jackson, Wyoming: Peter Woloszynski; mountain ranch mud room with stacked Navajo blankets: Peter Woloszynski; in the ranchland below the Snowmass ski area, a sled belonging to the Deane family used as prop for the film *North*, a Castlerock Production: Grafton Marshall Smith; capacious rustic ranch entry hall big enough for firewood, skis, saddles, designed by architect Jonathan L. Foote, table built by craftsman James Clair Sharp Livingston, Montana: Peter Woloszynski; Navajo rug, lasso, lariat, design by Marjorie Shushan, Aspen; David O. Marlow; p.148: courtesy the Aspen Historical Society; p.149: courtesy the Aspen Historical Society; pp.150-151: all three photos courtesy St. Regis Aspen Hotel; pp.152-153: teepee interior design by Cassandra Lohr: David O. Marlow; pp.154-155, top left: courtesy Art and Betty Pfister private archives; center: courtesy Lita Warner Heller private archives; top right: Kevin Lein; pp.156-157: David O. Marlow; p.159: David O. Marlow; p.160: David O. Marlow; pp.162-164 clockwise from top left: Aspen billiard room with panoramic view of Elk Mountain Range: David O. Marlow; mountaintop entertainment room in Aspen: David O. Marlow; Aspenites believe in tall-timbered big houses: Gibson Architecture: David O. Marlow; Navajo rug, Adirondack-style cabinet and a bed dressed by Ralph Lauren, design by Cassandra Lohr: David O. Marlow; hand-hewn log chairs accent a subtly elegant gray-hued Aspen living room: David O. Marlow; Jim and Betsy Fifield, who like to entertain in their home in a big way for such Aspen benefits such as Jazz Aspen and New Medicine: courtesy Betsy Fifield private archives; Dr. and Mrs. Russell Scott, Jr. with their grandson Andrew: Kevin Lein; inside the teepee designed by Cassandra Lohr: David O. Marlow; Ute chieftain, member of Aspen's original Native American tribe, circa 1900: courtesy the Aspen Historical Society.

Publisher's note: Every possible effort has been made to identify legal claimants; any errors and omissions brought to the publisher's attention will be corrected in subsequent editions.